NATURAL SUCCESS PRINCIPLES

NATURAL SUCCESS PRINCIPLES

By Jack Hatfield

New York

Natural Success Principles
Everything You Need to Succeed Was Inside You Before You Were Born

ISBN 978-1-60037-667-2 (sc)

Library of Congress Control Number: 2009929286

MORGAN · JAMES
THE ENTREPRENEURIAL PUBLISHER

Morgan James Publishing, LLC
1225 Franklin Ave., STE 325
Garden City, NY 11530-1693
Toll Free 800-485-4943
www.MorganJamesPublishing.com

EarlyJourneyFoundation.org

Natural Success Principles

Dedication and Acknowledgments

To my Life, Jonna Lil, and her mother
To my Roots, Ma and Pa
To my Future, each and every one of you

Foreword

Self-help books litter the shelves of every bookstore in America. People are searching their pages for ways to improve the quality of their lives. The reason people try so many books is simple. None is the right book. They don't offer the right help. They don't give readers the knowledge they seek so desperately.

This book is different. This book will help you find what you are seeking. This book is the right book. I'm not just saying that. This book is the answer to the questions you've been asking.

There aren't any promises of great monetary success in less than twenty-four hours if you read the book. This book offers no gimmicks or special prizes if you read it and then apply every single ounce of knowledge contained within its pages. There aren't any empty promises filled with crocodile tears that claim you will find it easy to apply any of the principles this book uncovers.

Instead, you will find simple truths. Truths so often overlooked, they seem to be revelations of a new and exciting horizon. The book shares methods of reaching goals and what you need to do to reach yours.

I didn't know these truths either. I had to learn them, just as you must learn them. At times, I have wondered at the ability my mind had to ignore what was right under my nose the entire time I struggled with the difficulties of life.

That's how simple these truths are. We know them, but no one realizes it because we dismiss the simple and jump straight to the expensive and complicated. It took a baby to give me this wisdom, but the truths she uncovered and made clear are truths that apply to every single person on the planet.

I hope you reach your goals and that the simple truths in this book contribute to your success. I hope you feel as awed as I do when discovering success hidden amid those things we tend to overlook in favor of society's preconceived notions. I hope there are moments when you consider the contrast between how complicated we make our own lives and how simply we began.

We can change our lives; we have the power to succeed; we have always had that power. We must find the way back to the truths we have forgotten in our hurry to rush through life. Slow down, smell the flowers, and enjoy the life you've always wanted.

CONTENTS

Introduction – Why Did I Write This?

Everyone has something or someone who has touched their life in inexplicable ways. It may be a loved one who took the time to spend with you when you needed it the most or an event that forever changed life as you once knew it. We consider them our miracles, our moments in the light of truth, and our saviors against the fiercest of storms.

I am no different. I had an event that changed my life and made it impossible for me to continue on the path I had once thought to be my destiny. My event also happens to be tied to the person in my life who began it with a certainty known only to angels. My angel is my daughter.

I know most fathers will be saying that they feel the same way about their children—that they are the little apples of their eyes, the joy in an otherwise bleak existence. Our children become the only things that matter. I think to a degree, they may be right.

My wife is just as special. However, my daughter turned my life around. It took Jonna to show me the truths I had long since forgotten. It took her rather tenuous start in life to get me to see the important things in life for what they are.

My daughter was born prematurely. She came into this world because of complications during pregnancy. Either she would enter our lives at the gestational age of twenty-five weeks, or I would find myself a widower without children. It was that serious.

Together, my wife and I made the decision that gave both of them a chance. It wouldn't guarantee that either would survive, but it gave them both a chance to survive. Death for both my wife and the baby was a certainty if we did not force my daughter from the warmth of the womb.

That is how Jonna began life. She didn't have fully developed lungs, she had fluid around her heart that stopped it twice, and she had only one kidney. Otherwise she passed the tests that parents are so fond of giving to their newborn children. She had ten toes and ten fingers.

Jonna lived through tubes and monitors in the beginning. Science tried to give her an environment that was as similar to the womb as possible. It didn't always work, but it did give her a spark of hope that life was hers to claim. And claim it she did.

Jonna fought to breathe, was placed on a respirator, dealt with being poked and prodded from every direction, and endured the pain that her existence demanded of her. She never gave up.

She hadn't read a book that told her how to survive. Jonna was unaware she had been given only a 30 percent chance to survive. She knew nothing of the conveniences we take for granted, but she didn't need to know any of those things. She had something better.

Jonna came equipped with unbridled Natural Success Principles she shared freely with the watching world. She taught me more in her first 130 days than anyone had ever taught me. She struggled against the odds and won. And she did it because of the gifts she brought with her. These are the gifts inside us all.

As I watched her battle for her right to live, I realized she was showing me how to succeed—really succeed. She redefined success for me, and she did it by reminding me of long-buried truths I once knew.

It was then I realized that everyone had these Natural Success Principles. It is with these principles we can achieve success anytime! We move away from them to satisfy a society we can't understand and want to fit into for our own purposes. As I watched these truths emerge, I knew I had to share them with others. I wanted to see everyone succeed in a natural way.

As I did this, my own definitions of success became more concrete. I realized I had been living under the definition society chose to give success and had been missing the most beautiful and miraculous parts of life because of it.

I decided I had to change. I had to take charge and take direction from the angel who fought so hard for life when it would have been easier and less painful for her to allow death to take her quickly.

I did just that. And now I'm sharing it with you. I want you to find the same happiness in life I have found by discovering what success is and how we get it.

As I watch Jonna now, I can hardly believe the amount of knowledge she gives to the world. She will always be my little angel, and I will always be her knight in shining armor. I will continue to live my life the way Jonna has shown me, and I will never miss another moment in it.

Share Jonna's gift with me and see just how good it feels. Let me uncover the most amazing feelings inside you. I promise you won't regret it.

Jack Hatfield

To get the most out of this book and to uncover your Natural Success Principles, use our workbook to help you with your transformation at *www.NaturalSuccessPrinciples.com/workbook.*

Chapter One

Not Just Surviving, but Thriving (True Success)

Everyone knows someone who beats the odds life stacks against them. Maybe it's you or perhaps a loved one. It might even be a complete stranger. Few people stop to think about why that person overcame more than most individuals see in a lifetime. No one concerns him- or herself with the reason. The only true acknowledgment comes in the form of recognizing what appears to be a miraculous event.

We accept that survival is an instinct that we can draw upon in a time of need. It isn't a far stretch to realize even more of the truth: the survival instinct we so readily accept is only a piece of some basic success principle drawn on some blueprint residing deep in our brains.

We are constantly perusing and exploring opportunities. Every action we take, every choice we make is the pursuit of those opportunities. We can see a difference only when we make decisions for success. Before you wonder if I'm just some crazy goofball, perhaps I should give you some background information that brings you up to speed on how and why my thoughts have turned down this unconventional alley.

My daughter Jonna was born prematurely—not by days but by months. She had a slim chance of living and spent 130 days in the hospital. Now she is living and thriving. Not to say we don't have our daily struggles with stuff other parents don't deal with, but for the most part, it is the best it could be every day. For day by day details on those

130 days, you can read *Blessed with Tragedy: A Father's Journey with his PreeMiracle*. She faced a mountain and struggled to climb it without any of the skills and knowledge that mountain climbers obtain before trying the same feat. Jonna hadn't read any books on choices or any that would give her the gift of miracles. Jonna did it alone.

As I watched her fight for every breath, for the right to live, I realized that she must be tapping a source of strength from somewhere. Since there were no outside sources for her to have drawn on, her strength had to be coming from an internal well—which meant that she had to have manifested it sometime after conception. Then I observed the other babies with the same plight. They were all doing the same thing. Some days were better than others. It was not an easy battle, but the babies were combating their circumstances just the same.

It wasn't uncommon to see a baby in the neonatal intensive care unit advance tremendously one day and give up the next. Some of the babies didn't survive, as is the way of prematurity. Prematurity is the number one killer of newborns. Jonna had days when we wondered if she would be able to pull through to see another one. She also had days when her progress astounded us completely. Even when it was hard, Jonna seemed consistently to choose to live.

I watched Jonna feel pain and struggle to take breaths. I watched her fight to live. Amid the pain, the anguish of living that was her world, she continued to hold on. When I observed her doing this, I first had a thought that believing in a survival instinct may not be accurate. I felt instead that Jonna drew upon an inborn natural success mechanism that we couldn't see. I also came to the conclusion, after comparing Jonna's struggle to other events in my life, that everyone has this system of natural success tucked inside them. But we don't all choose to use it, and some may not even know it exists.

Take an observation that came to me during a drive down a busy, dusty highway one day. As I drove, I listened to some motivational speakers, and I found myself absorbing some of the ideas they offered. As my eyes took in the scenery and the monotony of the road disappeared under my tires, I saw a stand of small, scraggly trees. One seemed scrawnier than the others. I realized that although the tree didn't have a survival instinct or even a sense of life as we perceive it, it did know to grow. Its only goal was to grow, regardless of the conditions facing it.

Before you decide I've lost my marbles, I'll agree that a tree doesn't have a brain. Or it doesn't have a brain as we have. It has a special code held within its DNA structure that dictates what the tree has to do, what purpose it holds. In that DNA structure, the seed of the tree is imprinted with the information to grow. So it does have a predestined Natural Success Principle as well, since growing for the tree is success. Not growing is death.

A seed, too, knows when success is obtainable for the tree it will become. If conditions are not conducive for the tree's growing, the seed will lie dormant until those conditions are met. This is similar to what I witnessed in my daughter.

Jonna did not enter the world under the most perfect conditions. Machines made it possible for her to survive. In a world filled with constant pain and agony, respirators would assist her breathing until the conditions were right for her lungs to function. Without aid from a bunch of tubes connected to a hissing apparatus, her body was ill-prepared to breathe as we know it. She had to have a feeding tube because her mouth did not understand to suckle as most newborns do. She had to learn it all. She had to have all of her conditions altered to survive. She had nothing in her world to give her what she needed, except what science had created.

This goes well beyond a survival instinct. The idea of a survival instinct presupposes that the conditions are ripe for succeeding at life. Each element of the idea of survival instinct relies upon all conditions for growth, for progress, for life being in place. For Jonna, this was not the case. She did not rely on the *instinct* to live, but rather the *will* to live. For her, the desire to have the life she was promised determined her fate. Jonna wanted what was rightfully hers and fought to get it, regardless of the difficulty or pain of that life. Jonna didn't just survive; Jonna succeeded.

The idea of these principles' natural foundation lies not on having the conditions properly in place, but rather on insisting on success, even in the absence of all environmentally necessary components for obtaining success. Success is built on the purposeful pursuit of desires through the use of the subconscious mind. Jonna didn't rely on instinct; she made a conscious choice within the confines of the definition of natural success to reach a goal regardless of the environmental conditions in place to achieve that goal.

This book will focus on the Natural Success Principles Jonna unlocked within her. With this knowledge, I discovered that we all have access to these principles, but what we do with them depends upon our own desires and our individual definitions of success. These principles are utilized in a different manner by each of us. As you peruse the landscape of society, you will also take note that you can see the different utilization within others. Some may only want to be a top cashier while some may want to be the president of an organization. The amount of strength we gain from our own store of these principles depends largely upon what we each define, based upon our desires, as success.

In short, we control our own success through our subconscious minds. No one else can do this for you, since each person's brain is different. So before we go any further, you need to decide what success looks like for you and how far you want to go in your life. If it isn't far, then this book will be of little value to you. It will help, no doubt. But if you only want to achieve small things, life is simple. This book will make that effortless. If you want to discover the full potential you hold, then this book will be the beacon that lights the way.

Chapter Two

Your Choice – Keep Growing or Die

The use of Natural Success Principles can occur at multiple times within one lifetime. It is what drives the type of courage that endures instead of the courage that is short-lived and spontaneous. If you want an example of this, and I'm sure you do, you really don't need to look beyond yourself for the answer to see the truth of this statement. The validity of it is so commonly seen that it is overlooked until you are in a situation in which it must be acknowledged.

Case in point: I must look no farther than my grandfather to see the result when Natural Success Principles are employed in the opposite spectrum of possibilities in the choices we make. He made a choice not to employ Natural Success Principles and gave up on the battle of life at the age of ninety-two.

Let me clarify that before anyone decides he was simply old. He was an old man who had enjoyed a very successful life. His life touched everyone he met and influenced those lives in a way that showed a positive edge. He touched my life in a way that propelled me forward toward my own destiny.

My grandfather took a fall, which is common in elderly members of our society, at the age of ninety-two. He cracked vertebrae in his neck, but did not sever the spinal cord and therefore had a chance of full recovery. The doctors told him and the family that this was not a life-threatening injury. It would, they conceded, be painful for him to breathe at times. They did say he would have to take it easy for a while during the healing process. They warned that he may not like the confinement his injury would cause in the short term. He had been in perfect health prior to the fall.

My grandfather did not choose to live after his injury. He willed himself to die because he was tired. His breathing did not become an instinct that he did daily. He simply stopped. He chose to stop. He wanted out of this life.

That doesn't make him a quitter, nor does it mean he didn't have a good life. He had a great life. He used natural success within himself many times over the years, but chose to stop using it after his fall. He was ready to pass on and made a choice to do just that.

Jonna chose a different path. She too had the choice of fighting or quitting. She even had odds stacked against her. Her lungs were underdeveloped; she was removed from the womb too soon for them to reach the maturity they required to work properly. She had pain; she had agony. She was confined more than full-term babies were. She faced her battle daily and strived to take breaths when no breath wanted to come easily.

Jonna chose to live. My grandfather chose to die. Both events were decided by drawing from Natural Success Principles and not an instinct. If it had been instinct, my grandfather would have lived to be even older than he was at the time of his death. His health indicated that he would. He had a great many years left in him, but he didn't have the desire to see those years after his fall.

Jonna had little of the environmental necessities that are required to sustain life, yet she fought to overcome those odds by using her Natural Success Principles. She wanted the years that were not guaranteed her, regardless of the pain that came with getting them. Jonna used these principles because she had no instinct that could operate within the parameters of her environment. The conditions simply were not available for her to succeed on instinct. She had determination. It was only through sheer determination that she overcame all obstacles.

Use our workbook to help you get started at *www.NaturalSuccessPrinciples.com/workbook.*

Chapter Three

Change Your Point of View, Perceive Success Every Time

Everyone goes through hard times. It is during these periods that many people, myself included, become aware of the Natural Success Principles that are held within us, awaiting our recognition and need for them. Some people choose to endure those more difficult times without utilizing any of the knowledge they already have in order to overcome their situations, and others make mountains look like molehills.

This raises some questions concerning the ability of people in general to be able to tap into their own Natural Success Principles in a constructive manner. Does it take a hardship to reach a point in which these principles can be accessed? Is the degree of the hardship relevant to that ability? Are other learned behaviors inhibitors to these principles? What impact do environmental factors or religious and individual beliefs have upon the accessibility of these principles? Is there a specific time in life in which these principles are easier to access than others? And can Natural Success Principles in others be recognized as such if the hardship is self-induced?

We are always perusing ideas and looking for opportunities. Natural Success Principles are opportunities waiting to be realized in opportune moments of daily life. This doesn't mean we can only access the power inside our own treasure chest of success during predetermined events, but rather that our awareness of these principles first occurs within the confines of a life-altering experience or hardship.

For example, a man who sits day after day eating orange cheese crunchies, playing a video game in clothes that seldom get changed while he complains of having nothing in his life of value can be said to be having a hard time. However, it is important to note that this hardship is self-induced and not necessarily one that will prompt a response from the well of natural success he holds. In this situation, the man has made a subconscious decision to fail, to be at the mercy of others for his existence. He does not actively try to change his life by altering his course of decisions, but rather wallows deeper into a dependency upon a social system of support than is necessary.

Perhaps this man's job is not satisfying. Maybe he makes little money at his job and feels uncompensated for the time and effort he puts forth. His family may not have the same opportunities as others in his way of looking at things. Yet he chooses a life of being a victim, of having little recourse in the outcome of any given situation.

What eventually happens with those who make a life of being a victim is ostracism. Friends and extended family fade away, unable and unwilling to be drawn into the same bottomless pit. As isolation further aids and justifies his moans of how unfair his hand in life is, the man relies even more heavily upon the charity of others. This sets his position within his perceived reality, and he begins covering up his Natural Success Principles to ensure success at failure. His goal, although made upon the planes of subconsciousness, becomes failure. He strives only to receive rejection and finds his success at making it happen. He is very successful at failure. Do you know people like this? Are you very successful at ensuring failure in things you do?

Another example of how your unaltered natural success can be used to achieve goals is to see how important perception is. Everyone perceives success differently, and the use of these principles will reflect that perception in the execution of the principles once awareness has been reached. It is important to note this fact in order to truly understand that we are in charge of our own destinies from the beginning.

A young man has just lost his job. He has a wife and a young daughter. There is another baby on the way. This man doesn't see the event in his life as a stop sign. He goes out every day and applies for all the jobs he can find, even those that pay less than his previous job. Nothing is out of the question: scrubbing toilets, cleaning kennels, working in an office, washing dishes. At each job, he acts enthusiastic to have the chance to work for the establishment.

At home, his wife begins to see what she can do to save money on expenses. She cuts back on electricity usage. She saves leftovers and learns to make casseroles. Instead of spending money on toys, she begins to make toys for her daughter.

The young man soon reaps the benefits of his job search. He is hired at the local shelter to clean up after the animals. His pay is considerably lower than it had once been in his previous position, yet he doesn't apply for state benefits or stop trying. In fact, he works hard and changes the way he lives to meet his new income level.

The young man has tapped into his Natural Success Principles. Instead of choosing to be a victim of his circumstances as we saw in the first example, this young man has become an active participant. He has taken control of the outcome by adjusting to the change without resentment. By choosing to be a part of the solution rather than a part of the difficulty, he has harnessed his idea of success and is using his store of these principles to ensure that success is sustained. His perception of success is one in which providing for his family through honest hard work is his priority, and he has utilized natural success to achieve it.

As you can see, the perception of hardship depended upon the one experiencing the hardship. This perception, and that of the definition of success, determined the outcome in the situations. These are both situations that are faced daily by a multitude of people. Some choose to overcome, and some choose to fail. To see either as not using natural success principles is incorrect as natural success is dependent upon an individual's idea of what success is. For Jonna, success was to live. For my grandfather, success was to pass into the next life. However, the decisions were made subconsciously while the actions taken to ensure the desired end were delivered consciously.

I know this concept is amazingly complex this early in a self-help book. Lots of books have lots of fluff at the beginning to make an easy read, but I have faith in you, dear reader. I expect a lot of people, and you get no free pass. So you can't give up when the going gets tough. You will not.

If you sincerely want to succeed, I know you will not fail to finish this book. You will continue. Look at you. Are you a quitter? When something gets a little tough, do you run crying to mommy, a beer, teddy, pet, etc.? No, you endure. You are my people. You are the people who make this country great and who make earth move for a reason. You look for ways to make things better. You endure. So because of this, we will continue. We will take the complex and make it understandable.

Chapter Four

Kill "Can't, " Destroy "Don't," Get Ignorant!

Some people find ways of excusing their circumstances or justifying their reasoning using fallacies that make absolutely no sense. In order to harness the true power within, the excuses must go. To think any other way is to be the spokesperson for the town idiot. There can be no excuses in order for change to come about. It's as simple as that.

My family's motto is "you've got to do what you've got to do." This holds true in all facets of life. I did what I had to do while going through the experience with my wife of our daughter's premature birth. My wife did what she had to do to give herself and our daughter a chance to live. Our daughter did what she had to do to live. It's a cut-and-dried concept, and I urge you to adopt it as your own.

I hear so many excuses on a day-to-day basis. Yes, I am aware that sometimes situations arise that prevent the outcome from occurring exactly as planned, but that only applies to certain situations, such as work productivity. It also has a set of extenuating circumstances that are found within that same realm. However, most excuses are not of this manner.

For example, let's take a look at battered women. I am choosing this group because the statistical information out there indicates that domestic violence repeats itself with the same women multiple times. This is absolutely insane, but it is a fact of our society. While I sympathize with the plight of these women, I find it hard to be openly objective when so many find excuses and justifications to return to these damaging relationships.

A young woman told me a few weeks ago that she was leaving her abusive boyfriend. She had plans to get an apartment, find a new job, and start anew without the black eyes and swollen lip from his fists. She complained that he hit her for any reason he could find, and that the occurrences of such abuse were increasing. First it had been once a week, then twice a week, then daily, and finally several times a day. She said she feared for her life if she stayed.

She managed to get a new place to stay—one that her new job would allow her to afford. The first week she was in her new home, I ran into her again. She told me how happy she was to be free at last from the abuse. She didn't make a fortune, but she was doing fine.

Two weeks passed, and I happened upon the young woman once more. She wore dark sunglasses and seemed to have lost the spark of determination that had been in her step the previous week. When I asked about the change, she told me that her boyfriend had moved into her new home with her. She had invited him to do so, since he promised he wouldn't hit her again.

Less than two days after he moved in, he began the cycle of abuse again. The sunglasses she wore were to hide the evidence. She quickly assured me that it had gotten better, though, and they were reconciled and doing great. I shook my head as I walked away in disbelief.

Don't tell me that the situation is better when it isn't. A hit, is a hit, is a hit. Whether it happens once a month, once a week, or several times a day, it doesn't matter. It still happens. The situation isn't better. The change isn't apparent. When the young woman chose to reenter this type of relationship, she chose to ignore what good common sense should have told her. Punching bags are found in the gym, not on a woman's face, regardless of the rate of occurrence.

Besides excuses, I hear a great many who feel a need to justify what they can't do. Having gone through the experience of my daughter's birth and knowing the sacrifices and changes I made to be a part of that event, I get more than a little irritated when I hear such things. Telling me you can't do something is just saying you don't want to try. Change isn't easy, so suck it up and go on. Let me repeat this differently. Getting out of a rut is difficult. It depends on the severity of the length, width, and depth of the rut as to its difficulty to drive yourself out of it. The longer, wider, and deeper it is, the harder it is to destroy.

This comes from hearing from another man whose wife is now facing a possible premature birth. He came to me saying that he didn't know what to do. He couldn't possibly take off work to go see his wife in the hospital. He couldn't miss work to be at the birth of his child. He also couldn't find the time to see his child if the baby were to have an extensive stay in the hospital.

I didn't have the time either. I made the time. My wife and my infant daughter needed me. In taking the time, I slept little, ate less, and prayed more than I have ever prayed in my life. I worked, spent time at the hospital, spent time with my wife and my daughter, and kept a blog while watching the tiniest of soldiers fight the mightiest of battles.

I couldn't believe the man couldn't figure out that the only thing stopping him was himself. He was choosing not to use any of his God-given Natural Success Principles in order to overcome the situation life threw at him. He didn't want to be involved, or he would have found a way. The old adage, "if there's a will, there's a way," is a forefront of these principles in that it creates the paths that lead to the answers in a situation that doesn't always have questions clearly stated. Your Natural Success Principles require that you override the instinct to abandon the seemingly hopeless. They require you to use everything you've learned, everything you were born with, to overcome the obstacles and locate a solution of success in a viable manner.

The choice isn't one of *can't* or *don't*. Instead, it is a matter of eliminating those phrases from your vocabulary and changing them to *will* and *do*. It isn't always easy, but the rewards far outweigh the effort. My daughter never thought, "I can't take another breath. I don't know how to live." She thought only that she must take another breath, and she would learn to live. She made those subconscious decisions without the benefit of years of experience in life or knowledge learned in books for the purpose of self-improvement. She didn't know she couldn't, and that gave her the strength to succeed.

So if you have ingrained in your consciousness that you can't; get ignorant about your abilities and tap into your Just-Born Principles and you will find a way.

Use our workbook to help you with your discovery at *www. NaturalSuccessPrinciples.com/workbook.*

Chapter Five

Ever Looked At Yourself in a Shiny Doorknob?

One of the first things that must be done to overcome a situation and tap into your Natural Success Principles is to change how you view yourself. Don't start off seeing yourself as a victim. Victims expect defeat, not success. Your expectations have a direct impact on the outcome of any given situation. How you see yourself forms the basis of your expectations. In short, break the belief system that you cannot change that which you did not create.

"It is a most mortifying reflection for a man to consider what he has done, compared to what he might have done."
—Samuel Johnson (1704-1784)

As I was driving down the highway one day, I saw the perfect example of this logic. I began to notice that the right lane of the highway wasn't moving well before I saw the reason why. As most do when we come across this type of situation, I thought at first that there must have been an accident. As I crested the top of a blind hill, I was amazed to see a car, obviously broken down, just sitting there. Its occupants, two good-sized grown men, were standing nonchalantly beside it. At times, they would wipe sweat from their brows as the day was very hot.

Now, not even a hundred feet away was a turn-off lane to exit the highway, with a gas station at its end. This was not a woman and child, but two grown men of substantial size. That is the most important thing to remember in this particular example. Instead of taking the initiative to push the car down the exit ramp, as all of its tires were inflated and this was an engine or gas problem, these men stood in one of the most dangerous spots they could and chose to be victims of their circumstances. They didn't even have the intelligence to abandon the car and go to the gas station on foot. They stood there, proclaiming to all how they perceived themselves by not doing anything to change their situation.

Beyond the fact that a car rounding the hill had only eight seconds to see the men and stop before hitting them, causing mortal danger, the car also congested traffic and created a situation of increasing the hardship of the men who owned the broken-down vehicle. I wanted to scream at the men that if they didn't like their situation, then they should change it. I realize that the weather wasn't the most forgiving, but being a victim to circumstance won't get you out of it, either. You must take the initiative and make the choices that change the obstacle in order to overcome the circumstance that stands in your way.

The men should have pushed the vehicle, as that would have eliminated the entire situation. They could have pushed it into the gas station's parking lot and then worked to discover the cause of the problem. Once that was done, they could have eliminated the problem or began to make concessions to rectify the situation by calling for a tow truck or ride if the problem was too large to be completely fixed in the parking lot. Not only would the mortal danger they had placed themselves in be eliminated, but the men would have also begun a course that would have changed their position in the situation from passive victim to active participant. They would have become part of the solution, not part of the obstacle.

At the very least, they should have removed themselves from the car and hiked the short distance to the gas station in order to phone for help if they had wanted to change the outcome in any manner. Instead, they were victims and trapped by their own perception of themselves. They ignored all possible paths to the resources of natural success because of their inability to see themselves surmounting their circumstances.

The consensus of the type of behavior displayed by these two men is one that the world owes them—that they are helpless and not to blame for any of the difficulties they face. Instead of finding success, they are to be pitied and handed solutions so they won't have to change the course of their lives. This is the mentality of the victim. Just as rape victims must overcome their situations and become advocates for themselves in order to heal and move on, so must all victims who choose to be victims change the course of their life, regardless of the degree of hardship they face.

Jonna, my daughter, could have chosen to be a victim. She could have decided not to live because it was beyond her and no one could or would live for her. However, something inside that tiny baby insisted that she would not be a victim of preeclampsia, which was the catalyst that caused her early arrival. She didn't actively cause her circumstances, but she actively participated in the solution to those circumstances to render a completely different outcome than would have been available if she had chosen to be a victim. If a tiny baby can accomplish this type of miraculous feat, why can't grown men on the side of a highway?

It all indicates that the only way to escape those things in your life that you don't like or don't want is to change them. That change has to come from within you. Don't stand by and allow circumstances to rule your existence. Take charge and do something about them. To do something is to become an active part of a solution instead of a passive victim who cannot help himself or herself. Natural Success Principles give you an ample supply of viable solutions that change the path of your life by overcoming obstacles and moving on to better things. If you don't like it, change it. It's as simple as that.

Use our workbook to help you start changing at *www. NaturalSuccessPrinciples.com/workbook.*

Chapter Six

Living Near a Volcano Can Get You Burned

Have you ever watched a baby? Have you ever noticed that babies are always smiling or laughing unless they have a true need such as being hungry, not feeling well, or having a rash? The answer is simple once the observation is made. Babies are born happy. Since we were all babies at one time, we were all born happy. It is the influences of outside experiences that causes the development of those emotions that center on unhappiness that cause the change. We aren't born with the inherent knowledge of their existence.

For example, let's examine two very prominent events in recent history. New Orleans has in the last four years experienced two very strong hurricanes of ill repute: Katrina and Gustav. The situations were both handled differently, but the ultimate outcome in the attitude of the residents of New Orleans was remarkably the same for each incident.

Katrina hit with a force that nearly destroyed any traces of the town of New Orleans. No one was prepared, making it one of the deadliest and most devastating hurricanes to hit within recent decades. The mayor of New Orleans didn't demand evacuation until it was too late to utilize the resources that would have been essential in such an operation. The government didn't require an evacuation of the area until the danger level was too drastic to escape. Busses stood empty and unused as flood waters invaded the city with a vengeance no one saw coming.

As the levies broke under the pressure of churning flood waters, residents clamored to find safety within the chaos of the storm. No safety existed. Repairs scheduled on the levies prior to the hit of the storm simply came too late to protect the people they were built to keep safe. To make matters worse, the devastation was too great for any help to really penetrate ground zero during Katrina for several days.

FEMA tried to compensate for the loss of organization by processing many of the refugees who did make it out of New Orleans prior to the storm's impact during the belated and ill-fated evacuation. However, they were not as prepared as they should have been for the magnitude of the storm and the number of displaced individuals and families who needed housing and assistance immediately.

Residents of New Orleans protested these failed efforts and demanded compensation for the lack of the organization and assistance the government bodies at both the state and local levels had readily available. They had lost everything and wanted someone to pay for that loss. FEMA met demands of many of these residents by extending the time allotted for housing assistance, even though many of the refugees had made the choice not to return to New Orleans. However, even that extension of services ran out so FEMA could remain in business for the next disaster that would require their assistance.

The state government did little to compensate its populace, as there were few resources available when massive reconstruction was the forefront of priorities for the state. Tourism in New Orleans is a major source of income for Louisiana, and rebuilding the city would recoup some of the damage to the state's financial situation.

While the National Guard and other federal agencies struggled to maintain a semblance of order, residents of New Orleans were making decisions concerning their futures as well. Many didn't return to New Orleans, too devastated financially to incur the cost of rebuilding, as a portion became the resident's responsibility. This created a mass confusion for New Orleans as it attempted to reassemble its populace. Forming a now broken whole out of the remaining mess of Katrina.

Four years later, Hurricane Gustav began a track that appeared to be a repeat of Katrina's path. Gustav was classified as a Category 3 hurricane, just as Katrina had been. The indications from the National Weather Center were such that measures were taken to ensure that Gustav claimed fewer human lives than Katrina. Evacuations were forced immediately. Busses ran continuously, taking residents out of harm's way in ample time to avoid a repeat of four years earlier. Programs not in place during Katrina were initiated to further stabilize the survival of New Orleans during Gustav.

When Gustav did finally hit land, the storm did minimal damage. Evacuees were not allowed back into New Orleans until the flood waters, which were not that deep, had receded and electrical lines were cleared from roadways to ensure safety in the return of the residents. Gustav did little more than wind and rain damage and resulted in minimal flooding. It spent its temper in the waters offshore, but did not feel the need to be that destructive onshore.

In short, people were uprooted from their homes and sent to shelters to wait out the storm in other states. Texas was a major player during this time as many evacuees came to the DFW area as a precautionary safety measure. Evacuations cost money, and evacuees were responsible for some of that cost. Many evacuees were responsible for all of that cost. They wanted their money back. Can you believe that? They felt that they were told to move and since the destruction was not great, it was the wrong call. Residents complained of over-cautiousness. What decision could you have made to satisfy people in this frame of mind? Can you satisfy people who think like this? I guarantee you, not one of them who has picked up this book has made it this far. They put it down before buying it. I hope they read the big, important chapter. They see it is as too complex and will highlight their otherwise bleak existence.

Just as with Katrina, the complaint became that officials in charge of hurricane preparedness were not prepared and did an inadequate job. In Katrina's case, the complaint was valid, as many of the victims of that storm could have been moved to safety if the governing bodies had acted soon enough. In Gustav's case, the complaint was unfounded.

No one can definitively predict the direct point of impact or the devastation that impact will have upon the face of the earth when discussing hurricanes. Just as with tornadoes, the only thing that science can do is predict a probability of course and force for these storms of mass destruction. There are no known methods of redirecting such a storm, nor are there methods of preventing or tracking these storms with deadly precision. They are a force of nature, and not one that man can control.

The cost incurred by the people in New Orleans is minimal when discussing Gustav, as the indications were that safety was indeed needed. Evacuation was done as a precautionary measure and is not a free method of prevention. However, for the peace of mind that there is a life to continue as removing a resident from possible danger in the wake of a hurricane means that the resident will survive the storm, the cost is well worth it. Had no evacuation been ordered as a mandatory safety effort, and had Gustav delivered what it promised, as Katrina had, many of these residents of New Orleans wouldn't be around to complain of evacuation expenses incurred during Gustav.

Quite frankly, most of America looks at it more logically than the people of New Orleans. Yes, hurricanes are terrible natural disasters that result in the need of assistance from programs designed for rebuilding and replacement of residents. However, if you're going to live in a valley that is below sea level and next to the coastline, then you should have anticipated the likelihood of such calamites in nature. Florida gets more hurricanes than Louisiana and manages to deal with a little better attitude. Why can't some people of New Orleans embrace a more positive attitude?

Floridians simply pack up the belongings, secure the structures of their homes as best they can, and get out of the way of the hurricanes that pound their shores with an eerie regularity. Keep in mind, this state also relies on tourism. If Florida can deal with it, then so can New Orleans. If New Orleans' residents don't like it, they can move. Otherwise, they should stop whining about that which is a direct result of their choice in living locations. Now before you start saying I am cold-hearted, listen—there are spots on this earth that are inherently more susceptible to a natural disaster. Some places are dangerous because of hurricanes, some because of tornadoes, and some because of volcanoes. If you live in a town like this, whining to me after a natural disaster occurs will fall upon deaf ears. You knew the risks beforehand; now don't be surprised when it happens. That is like saying, "I know this fire is hot, but I am mad as hell that my hand is burning after I placed it in there." What?

Jonna didn't have a choice in her birth or when it would occur. Her choice, I'm sure, would have been to remain in the warmth and security of the womb as long as possible, as is the way of all babies. Yet her attitude, even on a subconscious level, did not deteriorate to the point that she didn't try. She didn't behave as though life owed her, and she fought her battle courageously. She held onto the joy of life instead of the negativity of life, and it earned her a place in survival.

If you want to really change your circumstances, change your attitude. Find the joy you were born with and hang onto it. It's buried deep under the learned disappointments of life. It may be a little dusty from years of being unused, but it will still shine brighter for you than any cloud life throws your way.

Your current situation may not be perfect, but if you change your attitude about what is right versus what is wrong, you will be amazed at the difference.

Chapter Seven

9...10..Ready or Not Here I Come!

"**H**aving a positive mental attitude is asking how something can be done rather than saying it can't be done."

—Bo Bennett (1972-)

Set your priorities straight. This really does have an impact on your attitude and perception of your life. I can't stress enough that everything you need is held within you already. There is nothing you must go get to succeed, nothing to buy, and nothing that is stopping you but you.

I engaged in a casual conversation as I sat in a chair to have my hair cut, a normal activity for most of us. The lady who was cutting my hair asked the normal chitchatting questions meant to make time pass. The event was so ordinary that unless I hadn't been relishing the gifts my daughter gave me in teaching me that success was as natural as maple syrup, I would have missed the entire thing. I think this is what happens to most: We don't see what is right under our noses because it is there day after day without fail and without change.

"How are you today, Mr. Hatfield?" my hairdresser asked innocently.

"Perfect!" I replied cheerfully. "Just perfect."

"Perfect? I wish my life were perfect," she said, sighing heavily.

I gazed at her quizzically and asked, "Well, what's wrong with your life? What would you change?"

She sighed again, and then paused in her work to consider my questions.

"Well, I have bills piling up," she began. "And then there's the fact that I must work. Things just get hard, is all."

"So, do you think you can really eliminate an electric bill or maybe a house payment?"

She looked at me as if I'd lost my mind.

"Doesn't it feel good to work and give people something that makes them happy?" I asked.

The conversation continued as such for a few moments before I noticed a change in her as she worked on my hair, pausing often to talk. Then, something amazing happened.

"Well, I do have wonderful children," she said, smiling. "And most of my clients are smiling when they leave."

We continued to talk about her good points and what made her life special for several minutes after she was finished with my hair. In a matter of a few minutes—less than half an hour—she had gone from feeling as if her life were in constant turmoil and disrepair to finding the positive and realizing that she was indeed lucky to have the wonderful opportunities her life afforded her. Her attitude had changed simply because my attitude remained positive.

There is an old saying that a glass can be half empty and half full. If you look at life as being half full, your hand in life will improve because the negativity will be given less importance. Optimism isn't a learned behavior; it is a natural extension of your Natural Success Principles that are already there. All you must do is change how you allow yourself to feel about those things which can be perceived as difficulties in your life.

Jonna didn't see taking each painful breath as a pain half taken, but instead saw her efforts as a breath half taken. By having the fortitude to determine the more optimistic path, she didn't allow herself to be drawn into the negativity of her dire situation. She made the effort by maintaining a positive attitude throughout her ordeal.

"Positive anything is better than negative nothing."
—Elbert Hubbard (1856-1915)

Take a cue from the smallest among us and make your views help you instead of harm you in your quest for success.

Use our workbook to help you change your view at *www. NaturalSuccessPrinciples.com/workbook.*

Chapter Eight

"It" Constantly is, so Seeking "It" is Futile

Change. In a single word, the average person can feel a multitude of emotions. Many feel this type of impact when the word *change* is mentioned. Change, though, is the norm when describing life. Consider for an instant the number of changes to your life on a daily basis, and I'm sure you'll see the validity of this statement.

Change is the way we live life. Some changes are bigger than others, such as the birth of a premature child, the addition to a family in any way, the physical relocation of a home due to job or financial circumstances, and the discovery of a life-threatening or terminal illness. Other changes are small changes and go unnoticed, such as stubbing your toe and not being able to wear a favorite pair of shoes.

From our earliest moments, change begins to occur. Newborns experience a change in their complexions, their weight, their length, and a myriad of other trivial changes that are commonly seen during the growth process after birth. Children change in viewpoints as knowledge is gained and learned through experience as well as in growth patterns. Adults change in responsibility, financial security, ideas, and appearance as well. Change is all around us our entire lives. We cannot escape it. We cannot avoid it. Change simply is. This notion is even harder for me to swallow as recently, change became something people believed in versus something that was happening anyway, regardless of what you thought. They wanted change when they were getting it regardless of what they wanted. It is very strange, indeed, to conceptually feel for something that is happening all around you. It is like wishing for matches in a fire.

In light of the fact that change exists and is not something that can be eliminated from our lives, it is important to note how change gives us an advantage. If we could not change, if change suddenly ceased to exist, our current life situations would remain the same forever. For those of you who have a plentiful base upon which to draw, this would not be a hardship. However, what if your life situation is one in which you cannot afford enough food to eat, cannot provide a home for your children, or cannot get medical care for an illness? Without change, we would be stuck within the confines of our infant bodies and not ever experience the joy of growing in life.

That being said, it can also be reasonably understood that what we do with change in effect changes change. If change is embraced, then the results to our lives that the new set of daily circumstances brings will invariably be positive in nature. The positive impact may not be the change itself, but our perception of the difference and our acceptance of that which must be.

For example, you may not think it a positive thing to stub your toe and find yourself unable to wear a favored pair of shoes because of it. However, you might discover that the new shoes you were forced to wear based on a miniscule change in your life are far more comfortable than your previous pair. That is taking a negative and replacing it with a positive.

I didn't find the premature birth of my daughter a change that was completely positive. In fact, the fear that she would lose her life because of her early birth was a negative in the situation. However, the knowledge of simple truths so often overlooked that came from that event in my life replaced the negative impact of worry with a positive change in the direction my life would take based on what I had learned from Jonna.

Jonna's exit from the womb into the world was a major stress upon her frail body. She took that negative and replaced it with the positive of succeeding in living and the joy that it brings.

The point I'm trying to make is that change isn't always fully positive, but the positive can always be found in change. Personal disposition is a learned trait, and we can relearn to be more upbeat in our acceptance of change in our lives.

One way to do this is to see change as an opportunity instead of an obstacle. Natural Success Principles can assist us as we change our basic patterns of negative beliefs to more positive patterns in an effort to enhance our lives with more blessings. For me, Jonna is not the child without a chance. She is the child of hope that overcomes. She is not bound to my negative belief system that certain odds cannot be overcome. Jonna is a blessing in that she gives to me the strength to find the good in even the direst of circumstances.

Sometimes our belief systems, ingrained from our earliest years, are damaged by what life has dealt us. The first and most important thing we must do in order to overcome this hindrance is to embrace that change is a good thing. We must override our tendency to find the negative and focus on the positive to unleash what is already ours to claim. Change is our opportunity—the vehicle for success. Perception is the tool that causes change to become more important on our journey to success. Natural Success Principles are the building blocks of the road we must travel to reach success.

Change is a friend. Treat it like one to uncover what is hidden inside you.

Use our workbook to help you change correctly at *www. NaturalSuccessPrinciples.com/workbook.*

Chapter Nine

It Takes an Oar on Each Side of the Boat

A very important aspect of Natural Success Principles is the ability to recognize that assistance from another source, be it a person or a thing, is necessary at times. There is not a way in which you can do everything all of the time yourself.

In Jonna's case, she required two blood transfusions during her stay in the NICU. The blood transfusions were to increase a depleted platelet count in order to aid her in fighting infections. Infections are a high risk to premature babies, as even a simple infection or virus can be deadly to a weakened immune system that is overtaxed. Her body was seriously overworked in the sense that even breathing was a chore for Jonna. She didn't have the reserve of strength to continue meeting the demands of her platelet count at the time.

Couple that inability to produce enough platelets for her needs with the amount of tests that had to be performed in the course of her treatment, and the situation takes on an even more serious tone. Most tests were done from blood samples, which aided the low platelet count by necessity. Without the two blood transfusions she underwent, Jonna would not have survived. This is a simple fact.

Now, before you begin to question the validity of earlier chapters in which it was stated that Jonna chose to live, let's explain even more of this concept. Jonna did choose to live. However, without receiving and accepting some outside help, her choice would not have mattered as much. Her body could not produce enough of the vital components in blood to sustain her life alone. She needed the help in order to continue her path to surviving and succeeding when the odds were greater than they should have been for her right to live.

So, how does this relate to normal, everyday life? The answer is not difficult and is another one of the often overlooked facts of life.

In our society, independence is stressed. Responsibility is distributed heavily on those who possess this esteemed quality of independence. From an early age, we rear our children to be productive, independent, and upstanding members of our society. So ingrained is the habit of doing for ourselves that we overlook the delegation of responsibilities we carry as a weakness.

To get a promotion, you may have to have help. This may entail meetings and preparations for the position you are seeking with the help of another individual. It means a lessening in the line of independence.

However, using the help of another to achieve your goals is not a weakness as it is perceived to be. Strength is portrayed in those who know when to ask for help and when to accept that help in order to better their current situation. The assistance you get from another could mean the difference between remaining in your current position and gaining your goal of a more prestigious position with a bigger paycheck within your company.

Perhaps you know you have an idea that is astounding and should be turned into a book. You cannot do all of the necessary steps and processes of realizing your idea alone. You will need the help of a writer, unless you are one. Then you'll need assistance from an editor and a publisher. After that phase, a graphic artist is necessary for the cover design and layout of your book. Once that is done, marketing professionals and web professionals will be required to reach your goals. Finally, you will need the cooperation of bookstores to sell your book, both online and in stores.

The idea was yours, the belief was yours, but you must get the help of qualified professionals in order to see your idea reach fruition. Instead of being a vessel of the dependent victim, utilizing this necessary assistance gives you the opportunity to be independent in following your dreams and reaching a better place in your life that accomplishment brings to you.

Let's elaborate further and say that your new book is selling like hotcakes. It makes the national bestseller list. Now you envision it as a movie. You will again need to locate the help that will assist you in climbing your personal ladder of success.

The only weakness that you can truly show is a misplaced belief that you need no one and nothing to reach your idea of success. Help is a necessary component of any great achievement. By delegating responsibilities to those whose strengths are in the correct area of development at the correct time, you are enhancing your rate of success and empowering your own Natural Success Principles in the process.

Still confused on what this has to do with you? Let's break it down on an even more simplistic level. You are a clerk in a shopping center. A customer comes in and asks for assistance. However, there is a problem. You speak English and the customer does not. In order to do your job, you must get help in understanding the language that your customer is speaking. If you work alone, perhaps you could ask other customers in line. If you have a coworker, perhaps that person knows how to speak the same language as the customer.

You will find situations such as this and others that you require assistance in. Don't be afraid to ask for and receive help when necessary. This doesn't mean getting others to do everything for you, but rather learning your own boundaries and limitations in order to take full advantage of them. The outcome will greatly show the wisdom in your decision to get that push, that extra spark, to go from the idea to the reality in your dreams.

Also, do not get me wrong here when I say that individuality is anything but spectacular. Without the individual, discoveries would not be made, and most of life as we know it would not be. In fact, I am on a mission to revive the individual. You can read all about that in *Rise of The Individual* from my Anytime Success series.

A catalyst is the fuel for change. As we spoke of in the last chapter, change is an opportunity. Help is often the catalyst that takes an idea to full fruition. Accepting help when you are unable to do all aspects of a project completely alone will cause the change you seek to become a reality of your life.

Use our workbook to help you with your assistance at *www. NaturalSuccessPrinciples.com/workbook*.

Chapter Ten

Are You Eyeballing Me, Boy? (Visualization)

Jonna had to have two surgeries during her stay in NICU. For both of these, my wife and I were given consent forms to sign stating that we understood the risks and the possible outcomes. It was a standard procedure to ensure we understood that Jonna could die during surgery or have a multitude of other complications that we couldn't hold them responsible for as these occurrences were rare but did occasionally happen. There was no way for them to tell us that Jonna wouldn't be one of the few to experience such tragedy.

After I did research to find out what the surgery was supposed to do and how it would help Jonna, as well as if there were other ways to accomplish the same end, my wife and I signed the papers. The decision was made, and we had to wait and see how things would turn out.

Both surgeries had more benefits to Jonna than not doing them would have had. One enabled the lessening of needles, since they would be able to use an I.V. shunt to draw blood and give medications as Jonna needed them. The other destroyed portions of her retinas to keep her sight. The reduction of pain and the ability to see both offered Jonna an easier battle for her life.

The risks were there. She could have died during one of the surgeries. She could have sustained brain damage if she stopped breathing, so she was placed back on the respirator during this time. The scale was loaded with a world of "could haves" and a handful of "but look what you get."

We made the decision to take the chance because of the "look what you get." With that came the realization that how we envisioned the outcome would make a difference. The image of the result we carried had a distinct and important effect upon our perspective of the situation at hand and gave the strength needed to surmount the obstacles presented by Jonna's surgeries.

One of the most important concepts of Natural Success Principles is visualization. If you want to see a positive outcome, then you must envision a positive outcome. You cannot sway from that interpretation of the end result at any time or else the maximum benefit of positive thinking will not become your reality. I never visualized any outcome that would be negative. What good would that do? While the surgeries could be detrimental, those thoughts were never in my mind.

For example, if you have your eye set on a promotion at work, then you must visualize yourself already in that position. Let's say the position you currently hold is mailroom clerk. What you want is to become the manager of the mailroom. In order to do that, you must be able to first see yourself in that position.

Once you can visualize the position as yours, then you must begin to think about those attributes that a manager must have. Next, begin practicing those same characteristics of the job until they become second nature to you. During this time, you will be performing your job as a mailroom clerk without fail. It is in your body language, your speech, and your actions toward other employees that your ability to lead in a management position will become clear to your current superiors.

Once your boss notices that your work is well done and that you show potential for a position with more responsibility, he will begin to evaluate you as such. When the position you desire becomes available, your boss will likely think of you first. This leads to the realization of the visualization that created the proper attributes in actions while performing the work required of you. Finally, you will be offered the job.

Part of all success is the belief that you will succeed. Visualization of the outcome of any situation that you desire—regardless of the circumstances you currently face—gives you the edge you need to succeed. Natural Success is the same way. What you think you can accomplish, you can. What you think you can't accomplish, you won't.

There is an old adage that you are the only thing stopping you. This is a very valid statement, as your ability to thrive within your success depends upon your willingness to reach beyond your wildest dreams and make success happen for you. There is a measure of success that comes from thought alone because of how it compounds into your perception of yourself.

Use our workbook to help you visualize your future at *www. NaturalSuccessPrinciples.com/workbook.*

Chapter Eleven

More than Tough: Chewy, Even

One thing that you must learn is when to be tough. This doesn't mean you should yell, scream, and try to intimidate. That isn't being tough. I guess before I can tell you to be tough, I had better give you my definition of what being tough is.

"You become a champion by fighting one more round. When things are tough, you fight one more round."

—James J. Corbett (1866-1933)

When Jonna would have a bad day with low oxygen levels or forget to breathe on her own, or whatever she faced that day, I had to be tough. I learned everything I could about the situation, and I sat and continued to act as if everything were going to be fine. I'd give encouragement instead of giving in to the negative aspects of what could have happened in those times.

I am not saying that I sat blissfully unaware with a stupid grin on my face. I know all the outcomes from my studies; I just simply refused to acknowledge the negatives, as I did not desire their outcome. Also, don't think that you don't get negatives just because you don't think of them—but doesn't it seem like a better idea to try to see the positive and prepare for the negative?

Jonna was tough as well during those times. She struggled and continued to hang on to her tenacity to live life despite the difficulties she faced. It wasn't her body that was tough, but her soul and her will. Her drive to live was a form of strength that sufficed to give her success.

The body is a frail frame in which we live. It isn't tough in the sense that it is unbreakable. Skin tears, bones break, and organs sustain damage easily. None of these barriers provide much in the way of true armor. Therefore, being tough has nothing to do with yelling, hitting, or otherwise being physical to bring about desired results. To do so is to be weak, as the damage that can be sustained is great and easily inflicted.

Mental toughness is a desired attribute. Keeping your emotions focused on the positive in the face of the negative is being tough. Finding a way when none exists is being tough. Thinking that you will succeed and will gain the knowledge necessary to help you succeed is being tough.

It's similar to my belief on answering even the simplest of questions. If I am asked, "How are you today?" I answer, "Perfect." That usually gets the response of "I wish I could say that." You can.

Perfection to me isn't being without problems. It is not being physically stabbed at the moment, not being shot at in this instant, not being negative when nothing seems positive. That is what I mean when I respond that I am perfect to such a simple question.

The response of "perfect" is also an example of being tough. I am refusing to see any other state of being at the time. I am being tough in the fact that I will not allow my thoughts or words to show weakness. Showing weakness in words, thoughts, and actions will invariably end up showing weakness in the result. This, of course, snowballs into failure versus success.

I've been talking about perception in much of this book. All of the Natural Success Principles you already have depend upon how you see not only yourself, but all the situations and circumstances you face in life. If you are tempted to think that something might not work, it will follow in your words and in your actions. You make your success and the degree of it you reach; and you make your failures.

Jonna never thought about death as an option. She thought and felt life instead. I never allowed myself to believe that I would lose my daughter. I saw only images of her growing up happy and healthy in my home. Between the positive flow of our thoughts, along with those of my wife and the tenacity that Jonna showed in being tough of soul and mind, my little angel won her right to live.

Now, this doesn't mean that a positive thought alone is enough. Being tough also means learning to accept change and to bend with time. It means knowing when to use more forceful words to acquire the desired results and when to use softer, more sensitive words to reach your purpose. Being a hardass all the time won't help you succeed. Instead it will impede your progress.

Let's have an example, shall we? If your child is going to school and a bully picks on them, going to the school screaming and intimidating the principal will not help. Instead, take the knowledge of research on bullies with you and apply it. Explain what means you wish to reach and develop a plan with the school to reach it.

However, if your child is being beaten in the street before your eyes by an adult, step in and be a little intimidating. Become the hero you need to be with the situation.

In the workplace, you may hold a position that places you in charge. Your best friend is a subordinate employee that hasn't been performing up to par. After talking to this friend of yours about his productivity and performance at work to see if there are problems and finding none, you may be faced with having to terminate your friend. This would be a time to use strictness in the situation. Simply tell your friend that the company cannot continue to use him, and cite the difficulties of his performance as a reason. Do not begin to intimidate, threaten, or attack his character. That is not being tough.

Let's say that you have an employee who is seriously behind in her workload. You go to her and discuss the problem. You find out that her child is having a mental breakdown and she is facing having to hospitalize that child. Now, to complicate matters, this same employee also has to deal with the stress of mental problems of her own and that of her husband, as well as her other children who do not have problems. This is not the time to terminate the employee, but rather to find a way to help in the situation. Being tough here might mean lessening her workload by assigning another employee to help her. It might also mean encouraging the employee to succeed and to maintain her positive attitude.

In both these situations, the method used is different. One requires the hard-assed approach, as there is no indication of a reason for the poor work performance that is costing your company money. The second example shows toughness by displaying sensitivity to another's need and helping them reach a common goal. This nets you a more faithful and work-orientated employee that will assist the company more willingly in the future because of the treatment she received. There was an obvious reason for the lack of productivity, and therefore a solution that could be offered to assist the employee with success.

In Jonna's case, I chose a more subtle and encouraging method of assisting her as best I could. Yelling at her or dismissing her chances of survival would not have helped her. She had reasons for her difficulties; and therefore, solutions to them could be found.

This is how to be tough and remain in control of the situation that sits before you. It isn't a matter of physical strength, but of logical reasoning and problem solving. It isn't being a hardass in every situation. It is choosing which difficulties can be applied to a solution and which difficulties cannot. Difficulties that cannot be handled with a hard-assed attitude are those in which there is no reason for the problem. Those problems with reasons are waiting for solutions.

Natural Success Principles allow for those solutions to be found by delivering toughness in the necessary degrees and when necessary to overcome obstacles in the path.

Life happens. Be active in being tough and finding viable solutions to it.

Chapter Twelve

Algorithms, Architecture, Theoretical Physics and other difficult stuff.

Stress. Today, stress is cumulative in nature. There is stress in the workplace and at home. There is stress in the smallest to the largest tasks that we do on a day-to-day basis. Even cooking dinner or mowing the lawn seems to hold a minute level of stress.

"Some struggle is healthy. If you can embrace it rather than be angry, you can use it as your pilot light."
—Damon Wayans (1960-)

Stress is believed to be terrible by many, but in reality it serves a purpose. This doesn't mean that anyone can handle constant and unresisting stress for prolonged periods of time without feeling as if they are losing their grip on reality. However, some stress is good.

Let's discuss the reasons that everyone seems to feel stress is detrimental to the human body and psyche. There's the relationship of stress and illnesses such as heart attacks and stroke—and don't forget to add in the tremendous mental strain that stress can cause. If we only look at these aspects of stress, then it is indeed a bad thing.

Stress does have some salvaging attributes, though, that make it a necessary component when dealing with success. Stress gives an extra boost of urgency to those things we must get done in a given day. For example, if you have a book to write and the right amount of stress is applied, then you end up writing it before the specified timeframe. If you have the same book to write and too much stress is applied, then the book begins to run a little behind schedule. If you have the same book to write and no stress is applied, there is no urgency to finish it on time at all, and it is likely that it may never get finished.

Stress must be had in moderation, just as with every other aspect of life. In direct relation to stress, a release of stress is also necessary. This may come in the form a few quiet moments meditating or in an afternoon martini. Notice, I did not say forty martinis. I said *an,* meaning one. Just as stress must be had in moderation, so must the release of stress.

"Sometimes, struggles are exactly what we need in our life. If we were to go through our life without any obstacles, we would be crippled. We would not be as strong as what we could have been. Give every opportunity a chance, leave no room for regrets."

—Anonymous

Now that I've talked you in circles, let's give you a few examples.

In Jonna's case, just breathing caused stress for her. She struggled and strained to take each breath, but she continued to do it. Her release of stress came in the form of Daddy's hand—usually just a finger as she was so small—that she could feel brushing up against her face or nestled in the tiny palm of her hand. It calmed her, and she found the balance between the stress she felt and the release of that stress within my touch. In fact, sometimes she would get a little too excited to have a release of her stress, and I would be asked not to talk as it excited her and increased the stress that she felt when breathing. This is why balance is so important in stress. The release and endurance of stress must be in relation to one another in order for a balance to be found that engages in the positive management of stress.

I have discovered that if your job is high-stress, then you need to keep your home life low-stress. If your home is high-stress, then find a low-stress job. This is more important than I can stress. Families have crumbled, and lives have been reduced to shambles when all aspects of life are filled with high stress levels. I have seen this like there's no tomorrow. People must have a release from stress in some aspect of their lives in order to continue to thrive within natural success.

Stress that motivates and encourages one to produce greater and grander things is good, but only if there is an equal release of that same stress in relaxation. Your mind needs the rest of relaxation and the motivation of stress, but in balance. You must have an equal amount of both in order to be prepared for the next change that life has in store.

Change, as you know by now, is our mantra; and life is change. Nothing can stay the same. The reality of a completely stable environment in which change never occurs is only an illusion. Change happens in all moments of life. It can be subtle, or it can be overly obvious; but it is in everything around us at all times. It shows itself as a seesaw of stress and relief of stress. It is the only way life can be lived.

In order for your Principles to embrace the stress of life, you must allow your mind a release. It may be just a few minutes to prepare for the next moment of stress, or it may be a regularly scheduled weekend away. It should be something that you do on a regular basis. Exercising releases stress. Trying to meet a deadline while handling several life-changing events creates stress. If they are done in tandem and in balance, the end result is success.

If you wait for life to issue you an invitation to experience stress, and then issue another invitation for stress relief, you risk losing your opportunity to use stress to your advantage. Don't ignore change in order to save yourself. Change will happen. You must learn to go with it to find the balance between stress and release in order to unlock the full potential of your natural success principles.

Let's look at an example to help you see what I mean. You have a major project that has a deadline that is fast approaching in the next few days. You are well behind schedule because of life changes that could not wait. Now, this should motivate you to work harder and quicker in order to meet your goal of success. While this is true, you must schedule a few hours during this time to release the overabundance of stress that being behind on the project is creating.

If you go home from the job and find that your spouse hasn't cooked, cleaned, or otherwise assisted you with your needs in household duties, it adds stress. Then your teenage daughter comes in the door and is in an explosive mood, creating even more stress. Your day at work with the project has already supplied more than enough stress for the month. Where is your release?

If you must, go into the bathroom, pour yourself a bath, and soak for a while. Release the stress that has built up, or you may join your daughter in an explosive display of temper at your spouse while melting into an abyss of frustration. You become overwhelmed and cannot avoid meltdown status.

This incites your spouse, who is the brunt of your anger. The anger of your spouse feeds off your anger because there was no release for your stress. This causes your daughter to reach new levels of insolent behavior, and the problems within relationships truly begin.

In jobs, stress is responsible for a large number of the failures and capital losses that a company endures. Stress is also responsible for almost all of the successes of that same company. The difference is that employees of a successful company are encouraged and helped to find the balance of release that enables them to succeed. Companies that fail often do so because no balance of stress and release could be reached.

If you want to succeed, then let your Natural Success Principles help you reach the balance between stress and release. It will make a world of difference in how you handle accomplishments and difficulties along the way.

Use our workbook to help you cope with stress and make it work for you at *www.NaturalSuccessPrinciples.com/workbook*.

Chapter Thirteen

To Make the Balloon Lighter...do this.

Stress and balance can be located within Natural Success Principles when you find and keep the good relationships that fall into your life. You must nurture that which you wish to keep, and toss that which is not working.

By no means am I advocating that you jump from relationship to relationship as quickly and easily as you blink your eye. Each one that you encounter, whether business or personal, must be given a fair chance to determine which variety they are. This won't happen instantaneously; but it doesn't take an eternity either to know the difference.

When you develop a relationship, you need to decide how long you intend to test it with nurturing to see if it works well. This might mean a period of six months or longer before you can determine the workability of the relationship within your goals and timeframe for success. Some relationships may take longer incubation periods, and some may take less. It depends upon the nature of the relationship and your desire for the type of relationship that will enhance your life.

For example, if you have been married for fifteen years and your spouse provides you with support and love that lessen your stress consistently over that time frame, keep your spouse. Do what it takes to keep that relationship alive and well. In so doing, you are ensuring your success and happiness while embracing the changes that your relationship will undergo during the course of reaching your goals.

On the other hand, if you have been married for fifteen years and your married life is a living hell, be prepared to make a change. When you live in misery at home, it often carries over to all aspects of your life, and it can impact your ability to succeed.

I know this sounds tough and rather harsh. However, when you look at the big picture, it is a fact of life. Some things work out. Other things don't. You must take control of those things that aren't working and rid yourself of the problem. You must nurture and care for those things that are working.

Let's look at friendship. Some of your friends could actually be hindering your success. It takes a big, bold, and brave move to eliminate items in your life that impede your true potential—much bigger if the eliminated item is a friend. Look carefully at your friends; they may have to go. Do you have a loser friend? Do you have a friend who is a constant complainer? Do you have someone who is stuck on the hamster wheel of life, spinning and going nowhere?

"An insincere and evil friend is more to be feared than a wild beast; a wild beast may wound your body, but an evil friend will wound your mind."

—The Buddha (563-483 BC)

In the workplace, if you have had that same cashier job for the last twenty years and never been offered a promotion, you may consider the option of leaving the job to pursue more lucrative ventures. That's a long time to ring up items. Consider making a change, especially if you have trained all of your bosses. The kind of change is up to you, and the time for change is now.

Perhaps you need to change how aggressive you are in pursuing a higher position. Maybe you need to find a different employer with more opportunities. Maybe you need to go after the education that would ensure your promotion. You must evaluate the situation and then take action. Doing less is defining your success as failing to grow. Doing more opens doors that you may have overlooked until now.

Those doors might lead to a future that surpasses your wildest dreams of where you would like to be.

If you don't like your life, then do something about it, and make change happen.

Use our workbook to help you moderate your relationships at *www.NaturalSuccessPrinciples.com/workbook.*

Chapter Fourteen

Many Rains and Moons, but You Witness Only Few

If asked to answer the question, "What is our most precious resource?" what would your answer be? This isn't a trick question, but it does have only one correct answer:

Time.

Time is the only thing we have that cannot be regenerated or recycled. It isn't something money can buy. No one can create time, make time, or manufacture time. Time is truly a resource that is to be treated as if it were a treasure made of the finest porcelain china. It is worth more than all of the gold in the U.S. Treasury Department. Nothing is more valuable than time.

Now, before you decide this isn't true, think about how you can make time. When you discover the secret of it, I hope you feel compelled to share it with the rest of us. It is the one thing we all want more of, that we want back, that we want *period.*

I know many think that time is money, and therefore money is time. This may be the cry of business, but it isn't a phrase that is meant to be taken literally. It is meant figuratively and as a symbol as to the value of an employee's time to the company.

I sat with Jonna for over twelve hours a day. It was the most important time I spent and the most precious gift I could give her. I am often asked how I could do that, but I always wonder, how you could not? Nothing else would have helped her, but my time gave her a sense of security that she needed in order to help in her survival.

If I had spent that same time making money, I wouldn't have been helping my daughter. Further building my bank account would not have provided her with the sense of emotional security or the companionship of a parent during her greatest hour of need. Building the world of technology would not have provided her with the sense of love and encouragement that she needed.

That's not to say that technology and money didn't play important roles in Jonna's recovery—but they were money and technology already in existence. Making more would not have given her a better shake in life. Leaving her side would not have helped Jonna in any way. I gave her what I had to give—the one thing that she needed the most from me, and that was my time.

Consider what happens when you realize that a relative is dying. The first impulse we have is to go sit beside them as they pass. Why this is so is rather confusing, because many times we did not visit or spend time with the relative in question during the years preceding their death. Our fascination with this comes from an innate realization of the fact that time is irreplaceable.

Instead of waiting to share your time until the last moments of a business venture with someone or beside the bedside of the relative in question, spend it with them when it matters most. When you give your time to someone, do it with the intent to give them a gift. When someone spends time with you, appreciate their time for what it is: Their most precious resource to give.

Along with this concept is the ability to prioritize your time. When Jonna was in the NICU, she was my priority. I didn't worry about my job, my business, or what society thought of my sudden absence. She needed me, and I was there. Be there for your priorities, whether personal or business. Spend your time wisely, for you won't get another chance to spend that same block of time again. It will already be gone.

In the journey to your success, this could mean spending time on those things which are giving you something back. It is all tied to reducing stress, releasing stress, nurturing good relationships while ridding yourself of bad ones, and making the most of your most precious commodity. Time is not to be wasted. Don't waste yours or anyone else's if you plan to reach the highest point you wish to obtain. Find the ways that time will be best spent, and then spend it accordingly.

Allow me to illustrate my point once more; if you sincerely look inside yourself and discover your definition of success, you will likely find out that "time" was what you wanted all along. It was hidden among these likely happy moments derived from your "success":

A. Wake up my children every morning
B. Show my family incredible vacations
C. Go explore this wonderful world
D. Be there for my children
E. Tell my parents how much I appreciate them
F. Help others at the food bank

As you can see, hidden ever so slightly in every wish above is more time. The most important thing you can have is more time. While you can't get more, you can get to where you use more of your time doing the things you *wish* to do, instead of the things you *have* to do.

"If we take care of the moments, the years will take care of themselves."

—Maria Edgeworth (1927-2002)

Use our workbook to help you evaluate and make the best use of your time at *www.NaturalSuccessPrinciples.com/workbook*.

Chapter Fifteen

Runoff is Not Always Sewage

If you want to unlock your greatness and the secrets of your own personal success and make the most of your time, find the people who exude greatness. When greatness drips off of someone, then they have found the secrets of Natural Success Principles within themselves and can unlock them in you.

The doctors and nurses who took care of Jonna were the catalysts for me finding my success principles. The care and love they poured upon those infants in NICU was incredible. These babies weren't their own children, but they were treated as if they were. These people fought to keep these children alive and to give them more than just life. They fought to overcome the obstacles that often overshadowed hope, and they succeeded.

We cover up and bury the natural success inside ourselves so well that sometimes it takes another whose natural success has been revealed and radiates from them before we can locate where we hid our own. It isn't that we don't want to use natural success, but that it becomes something we must find once we've sheltered it away.

The best use of time, which is our greatest commodity, is to find and learn from those who have discovered the secrets in natural success. The doctors and nurses had a job to do, yes, but most went past job descriptions. I am telling you, this is the highlight of human existence—the compassion within. These weren't their children. They didn't have to try so hard, yet many of the doctors and nurses that cared for my daughter went beyond the call of duty to help her survive. They did it for all of the babies in the NICU.

It didn't matter how tired or busy they were. They gave their time and their greatness to everyone who needed them at the time. They gave it freely and with joyful hearts, which inspired the discovery in me and in others. It was through watching them, observing Jonna, and realizing that life held more success based on our own choices in how to use our resources that I finally understood that we are all equipped to succeed. We already have everything we need to succeed.

It was with this realization that I discovered the simple truth of Natural Success Principles. While we already have everything we need within us, few know about it, and even fewer can access it at will. The trigger for using natural success is different for each individual—as is the definition of success. Still, all of the success principles that we need are inside of us *before* we are born. I am the expert witness to this.

There are books upon books out there on self-help. Gurus prescribe a multitude of regimens that supposedly deliver instant success. However, success isn't an instant process and cannot be turned into an instant process. Success is the well within ourselves that tells us what we want out of life and how to get it. It is a series of events based upon the desires of the soul and the will of the individual. Natural success is change, and change is life. Embracing change allows for success; facing change allows for learning success. Together, these principles work in tandem to create the perfect success for each individual person.

No amount of money spent on seminars and other events that suggest weird and rather inconvenient regimens will gain you the success you deserve. Only surrounding yourself with the processes of natural success can give you that. Look for those people who can help you unlock yours. They are all around in our neighborhoods, schools, hospitals, and homes.

The ones who are already using their success principles are waiting for you to ask and to learn from them how to unlock your own.

Use our workbook to help you with your mentors at *www. NaturalSuccessPrinciples.com/workbook*.

Chapter Sixteen

Remember Cubby Holes in School?

In order to fully appreciate and reap the benefits of your success, you must learn to prioritize. This applies to every decision, every moment of your life. You cannot decide to prioritize half of your life's decisions, not prioritize the other half, and still expect to see results that are incredible.

When Jonna was in the hospital, there were several decisions that had to be made that would greatly impact her life. Whenever possible, I asked for an overnight period before the procedure was to take place. This was so that I could research and find the best possible answers to my questions that would give Jonna the most advantageous benefits. I started doing this when I discovered how much I could learn from that research during that overnight period. I made that decision a priority.

I realize that some decisions had to be made spontaneously. There were even a few that weren't to be made by me or my wife, since circumstances and Jonna's difficulties made the decision for us. Still, when it was possible, I chose to learn as much as I could in a twelve-hour period to make an informed decision.

In the scheme of things on your way to reaching your natural success, you must do the same thing. This prioritizing of decisions doesn't apply only to the large ones in our lives. It applies to every moment of our lives and to every decision that we encounter.

You realize that picking up little Johnny from school each day is important. It should be one of your top priorities. Taking little Suzy to the doctor to clear up that rash is another big priority. Getting food to cook for dinner and paying bills necessary for your household all hold great importance on this scale.

However, there are many decisions that we make that don't deserve our time, since the result of those decisions yields nothing in return. Nosy Mary down the street doesn't really have to gossip about everyone in town. The time you spend allowing yourself to hear this gossip is time you have lost with little or no return for your investment. Nothing in the gossip session will yield you success or allow you to grow in a positive manner toward the success you seek.

Your best bud Jim doesn't really need to whine about being passed up for another promotion. Instead of wasting your time, he should be trying to unlock his own natural success and figure out why he is consistently passed up when it comes time for advancements. Perhaps his time and yours would be better spent if he weren't allowed to wallow in his own sorrow.

Before you think me cold-hearted, I am not saying to be uncompassionate. I am telling you that you must locate the parts of a relationship that are beneficial to you and avoid those parts that aren't when making the decision of how to spend your time.

The return of what you get out of the relationship is always at the forefront of importance. If you aren't receiving anything of value, why are you paying top dollar with your time? Remember that when something isn't working for you, it is working against you. With that in mind, consistently seek those relationships that give back to, instead of take from, your store of time. Time is the only resource you can't replace or make new in this world. You can't breed it. Don't waste it.

I didn't waste my time when Jonna was in NICU. I spent every moment as wisely as I could to ensure her success. Her success marked my success and the success of the doctors and nurses that took care of her. Time was used efficiently and for gain, as it should be. I didn't gossip with the doctors, nor did I listen to the nurses discuss what television soap opera had the best-looking men. I do have rather friendly discussions with them now, after we are grown and the crisis is averted. I did gather every piece of valuable information from them to help me unlock my own Natural Success Principles in order to grow and learn what I had to for Jonna.

As you go through your day, ask yourself what you are gaining from your decisions. Then weigh those answers with your goals, and see if there is a common link between the two. If there isn't, change your decisions to increase your success.

Use our workbook to help you prioritize every moment at *www. NaturalSuccessPrinciples.com/workbook.*

Chapter Seventeen

Max Out the RPM Sometimes; Clear the Gunk

"**S**uccess is the ability to go from one failure to another with no loss of enthusiasm."

—Sir Winston Churchill (1874-1936)

Testing the limitations that you have on a constant basis is extremely important to your success. It is a natural process that begins the day you are born and ends only upon your death. Testing your boundaries causes you to grow in ways that you would not have otherwise. In fact, testing yourself is an impulse that cannot be controlled entirely by you, especially in the beginning of life.

When you were little, your mother probably told you multiple times not to touch the stove. She more than likely gave you a reason. The stove is hot; don't touch it. In your mind, you heard it a little differently. Her gentle warning became a sort of challenge to you. Could you touch it before she said not to touch it? Eventually, you tested your ability to see if your mother was correct and touched the stove.

If you were unlucky enough to touch it while it was on, the stove probably burned you. If this was the case, then you jerked your hand back quickly and began crying, both from hurt and surprise. You more than likely became aware of the stove as a thing not to touch, just as your mother had told you.

If you were lucky and touched the stove when it wasn't on, you learned that the stove wasn't quite as hot as your mother claimed it to be. This may have taught you that your mother wasn't right all of the time. It may have even led to the beginnings of questioning vocally your mother's statements. This, of course, would have led to you finding out why you don't test the limits of back talking.

From this example, you can see that testing is a natural and normal process that we have done since the day of birth. It is also a growing and expanding process. The first tests were those of taking breaths, blinking eyes, and moving our bodies. From there, they simply become more complex, but the testing continues.

Jonna tested her body often during her stay in the NICU. She would pull her knees up and squirm. Her little back would arch. She tested her movements often, even though it lowered her oxygen level and exhausted her in the process. For her efforts, her reward was an extended nap.

Now, if she hadn't tested herself, she would not have learned that she could move. She would not have realized that her body responded to her in the way she wanted it to. Jonna would still be lying still and silent if she hadn't discovered her boundaries.

As with all testing, once you've done something one time, you should see if you can do it better the second time. Jonna tried that, too. At first her knees only lifted an inch toward her chest. As she continued to try the action, though, it became more pronounced, and she got her knees closer to her chest.

Once you realize that testing is necessary to move you forward through life, you must also become aware that limitations and boundaries shift and change. Just because a test of yourself revealed a boundary when it was first attempted does not mean that the limitation you located will remain constant throughout your life.

For example, the first time you attempted to write the alphabet, your letters didn't form words, and they weren't the exact copy you thought they were. Some may have been backwards or of a new shape altogether. As you practiced, which is a form of testing, you learned to make them just the way the letters on the chart your teacher showed you looked. With a little more practice, you discovered that writing them in particular orders rendered words. This continued on, and you discovered that you could make sentences. From sentences, you progressed to paragraphs and onto stories.

"Success isn't permanent, and failure isn't fatal."
—Mike Ditka (1939-)

At each level of learning, you push the boundaries of the limits you had before and stretch them. Each time you stretch a limit a little farther, you grow. If you don't test the limits you currently have, then you will never advance beyond where you are right now.

Part of this concept is based in your attitude about your life. If you believe you can, you can. Remember the story of the little tugboat that could. He thought he could, and he did. Use visualization to enhance your testing, and you will find as much success as that little tugboat did. He pulled himself along the mighty river upstream against the greatest odds. If he can do it, so can you.

On the other hand, if you think you can't do something, you're right. Visualization is a very big part of success, and if you can't see yourself doing something, you won't test yourself to do it.

I have seen people build businesses out of nothing. They didn't have any business experience, nor were they particularly gifted in the area of that business. One such business started off as a mere list on the internet. It was nothing more than a group of people on the internet sharing a common love for a particular theme. The whole concept of the group was how to save money doing what they loved.

Somewhere along the line, the founder of this group decided to test the limits. She took her idea of running a business from an idea group and moved it into reality. When I asked her how she had managed it, her answer said it all.

"I didn't know I couldn't."

At the time, her revelation didn't mean much to me. I thought it an amazing feat, but I didn't grasp the full power of her words. She didn't know she couldn't. That meant she had unleashed her Natural Success Principles and had drawn up a gem. Her attitude toward her achievement was one that said no one told her she could not do it. She saw herself as the owner of her business, found others who would benefit her in her endeavor, and then tested her ability to make her dream a reality.

That is exactly what you must do. Test your limits on a constant basis, and adopt not only that change is life and life is change, but also the philosophy that you don't know you can't do something. If you have something you want out of life, you must abandon the idea that you can't. You must decide that this venture, this dream, is unique only to you. That means it's untried and untested. You don't know you can't do it. The only way to find out is to test and try that limitation.

So go out there and test yourself every chance you get. The more testing of limitations you do, the more you grow. Just don't take it as a license to test the limits of the law. The only testing that matters is that which is of a personal nature and not of an illegal nature. If you do get the idea to test legal limits, keep in mind that you will end up in prison. It has been done before, and it never works out well for the one doing the crime.

Use our workbook to help you max out your RPMs at *www. NaturalSuccessPrinciples.com/workbook.*

Chapter Eighteen

Ignorance is Possibly Humanity's Downfall

"Learning is like rowing upstream; not to advance is to drop back."
—Chinese Proverb

I want you to take a moment and think, if you will. Think of everything you have ever learned in your life. Think of the sources of that learning, even at the toddler stage when you were learning your ABCs. Bring to mind the college courses you just took on anatomy and physiology or of that basket weaving class.

Now that you are thinking of everything you've learned, I have a question: Where did it come from?

The wisdom of the ages that has been placed in books is where we start. Everything we learn has its primary basis in a book. There are exceptions to this, as some things are innately known with no known origin. You didn't learn to breathe from a book, for example. However, you did learn about lungs and how they functioned to keep the body supplied with oxygen from a book.

Your colors, numbers, and letters all came from books. You have been learning since the time of birth and will continue to learn throughout your life. Each day will bring a new morsel of knowledge. Sometimes the bit of knowledge you gain is so small that you don't notice it at all. Other times the information is so profound that you cannot get over how you came about it.

Learning happens naturally and without effort in this manner. There were times in my research as I desperately searched for answers for Jonna that I came across things the doctors found interesting. They were experts in prematurity, but they hadn't seen every single study. The studies I brought in, while they didn't pertain to Jonna, were of interest to the doctors, since reading them was a method of learning even more than they knew before.

The reason that learning is so important to your success is really simple. The more you know on a subject, the more you increase your opportunities for success. I have a background in computer technology. While I know a great deal about computers, what I currently know will not match the amount I will know in another five years. I know some of you are thinking that the reason this is so is because technology changes so quickly. This is true—but so does every aspect of life.

Let's take something as simple as running a vacuum cleaner. In the early days of cleaning, we used a broom. Every surface of the floor was swept, regardless of what kind of surface it was. When the electrical vacuum cleaner came about, housewives had to learn a new method of cleaning their floors. As the years progressed, we discovered how a vacuum could remove allergens in the air. Learning took place as housewives began to look at their environment differently. Not only were dust and dirt a problem, but tiny allergens could harm their families. Instantly, housewives wanted to know more about these invading allergens.

Today we use filters to capture the allergens with more powerful suction on the vacuums, and we no longer change the bags on the vacuums. It isn't necessary, as many models no longer have bags to change. With each improvement of the vacuum, housewives had to learn a new method of using them. It was a changing process that enabled the housewives of today to know more than the housewives of thirty years ago about how to operate and use a vacuum cleaner.

As you can tell, learning takes place in everything, from the simple to the complicated. We are the drivers for that learning, as our quest for knowledge expands constantly. Through the expansion of knowledge, we form opinions and test boundaries. We decide to think we can, and we can visualize ourselves knowing more in twenty years than we do right now.

Learning is the visible part of unleashing your Natural Success Principles. It allows us to explore the power within us and to expand on that power. The more we learn, the more we can release the success inside that is waiting for us to discover it. Learning is the discovery that unlocks in us the necessary components of our success to allow us to reach heights we didn't even know existed. You have to know that you need to learn. You have to want to learn.

"To be conscious that you are ignorant is a great step to knowledge."
—Benjamin Disraeli (1804-1881)

The other great aspect of learning is that it happens even when it isn't formal. You will learn and grow without ever having entered a school. No one has to tell you to learn; it is an automatic function. You can't even be taught how to learn. Your mind already knows.

If you think I just fell off my rocker, then consider the smallest among us. An infant such as Jonna doesn't have a clue about school. They don't even know it exists. Yet these infants are learning on a daily basis. They are learning to live, to blink quickly or slowly, to smile, to laugh, and to love. They learn to cry when they discover pain or sadness. They learn from the moment they enter this world, and no one teaches them.

A parent can show a child such things by displaying the behavior when appropriate triggers are in place, but a child already has everything he or she needs to do them without the parent. For example, a parent's love for a child is the strongest love that there is. The child may feel that love, may enjoy that love, but that doesn't teach the child to love. The child already has the skills necessary to display affection and feel love without a parent's guidance. A parent only shows how to display that love so that it is understood by others.

"The beautiful thing about learning is that no one can take it away from you."

—B.B. King (1925-)

Learning is the most important thing we can accomplish to reach our full potential. Ignorance has caused humanity more harm than anything else on earth. It is worth the time invested to learn all you can about the things that are most important to you. Doing so will help you reach your goals and realize your dreams.

Use our workbook to help you learn and grow at *www. NaturalSuccessPrinciples.com/workbook*.

Chapter Nineteen

Without This, the Rest Means Nothing

"**S**afeguard the health both of body and soul."

—Cleobulus (ca. 500 BC)

When Jonna was in the hospital, she had to go under a blue light in order to help her use some of the vitamins in her body. In the process, she gained a tan. While I can't be sure that there is a correlation between that time in her life and now, I can say that Jonna has grown to adore being outside.

The blue light is a type of UV light. It is similar to the rays of the sun which help us process vitamin D. The lack of vitamin D will produce a condition known as rickets. Other vitamins are also dependent to some degree on UV light. If there is no UV light exposure, then the vitamins cannot be broken down and used by the body correctly.

Now, this seems to be in direct contradiction to the pronouncement of health officials concerning the dangers of the sun. UV light has been linked to certain types of cancer, but the lack of any UV lighting will create just as deadly of a situation. The key is to balance your exposure to gain the benefits UV light has to offer while avoiding the negative effects.

This same idea applies to diet. If you are going to eat red meat, fine. Just don't eat only red meat. Take the battle of the new "fat" issues.

Fat, it seems to me, has as many studies which tell you to eat it as it has studies which tell you not to eat it. We know it is vital. Every choice you make should be one of moderation, not excess. Excess has consequences that are sometimes not desirable.

For example, there is a condition known as rabbit starvation. It got its name from the diet of the people who suffered from it. The disease, which really isn't a disease but a deficiency, came about after a group of explorers in the Arctic region attempted to survive on lean meats alone, mainly rabbit. It wasn't something they did on purpose, but no other food was readily available in the area. Nineteen left for the expedition. Six returned.

Because of their diet of lean meats, they slowly starved to death. They ate every night and had a good amount of the meat, but it wasn't in the right proportions nutritionally to sustain life. Fats and carbohydrates are necessary for survival of the human body.

Some symptoms of this condition are feeling lethargic, a hunger that cannot be sated by anything but fats, and diarrhea. While the choice of diet was due to circumstance and not a willful decision, the result was the same. If the body does not get what it needs in the amounts it needs, it will die.

My own diet is full of what the experts claim to be death traps. I eat all of the wrong foods fixed all of the wrong ways. However, I balance that with foods that are good for me and fixed in manners that promote health. The end result: I am very healthy, despite what should be an atrocious diet that creates a multitude of maladies.

I'm not saying to never go on a diet or to ignore every piece of advice given by your doctor concerning your diet. I am saying that you must find a balance in your choices to remain healthy. Health and diet are not necessarily Natural Success Principles, either, but balance is.

"Quit worrying about your health, it will go away."
—Robert Orben (1927-

In order to be successful, you must find the balance between excess and denial. Too much of anything can turn a good thing into a bad one just as too little can. You must search for and locate the necessary balance in your life so that you reap the benefits of health.

The reason I have mentioned health is really elementary. If you don't feel good physically, how can you feel good mentally? Your attitude directly affects your ability to find success, and balance has a direct impact on your attitude.

So many of our Natural Success Principles are directly related to the others in a profound way. You must find a balance so that you don't cancel out the abilities of one over the other. It takes them all to reach the true measure that is success. Take the time to find your balance, and then maintain that balance throughout your life.

Find out how to get healthier through good nutrition and other healthy habits at *www.NaturalSuccessPrinciples.com/Health*.

Use our workbook to help you with your overall health at *www.NaturalSuccessPrinciples.com/workbook*.

Chapter Twenty

Pools Use Filters to Make the Water Clear

We've talked about a lot of things that construct the Natural Success Principles. Perhaps I should also talk about a concept that will make it easier for you to follow the process of building your success with as little difficulty as possible. In actuality, this concept is a form of a principle, as it is a way of doing it.

We discussed the need to prioritize. One way that you do that is to filter the information that you receive. This applies to all information that your brain processes in any given day at any given moment. Some of it will occur without you realizing it is happening, such as the way it did when you were a child. Some of it will take a conscious effort to maintain a filtering system to avoid an overload of unnecessary bits of information.

When you learned about the stove being hot, you didn't keep the full experience. You probably don't remember having made that first reach for the stove. You might not remember the day, the time, and your age at the moment of discovery. What you remember is that the stove is hot. That was the only truly important information within the discovery you made. It created a definite course of action throughout your childhood when you encountered another stove. It also had an impact on your respect for the stove as you began to learn later how to use that hot thing to your benefit.

Children do this without a second thought. They don't analyze anything that they filter, and all of the information filtered in the early years happens automatically. It is only as adults that we begin to consciously separate fact from fiction, important from unimportant. It is a process learned in school and fostered as we become aware of critical thinking skills and logic in assessing the possible outcomes from different scenarios.

We begin to realize that the news is biased in the fact that not all angles are shown. This begins the recognition of fallacies within facts and allows for more filtering of information. We no longer believe everything we read or hear. We question facts and make discoveries that advance society while increasing knowledge.

Some people don't seem to understand that the media and our world in general do not hold only relevant information. Much of what we are bombarded with on a daily basis has no relevancy at all to our present situations, nor does all the information have a place in future relevancy.

Take this small idea for a moment and see if you agree with it or not. It will tell you a great deal about yourself and your current filtering abilities, as this is an example of the type of statement that encourages herd mentality when individual growth is more desirable:

All women can have babies. Only women can have babies. Therefore all women have babies.

In this example, it is obvious that you need to work on your filtering abilities and perhaps your reasoning skills if you think this is true. While the first two statements within the main statement seem true and seem like relevant information that you may need one day if you plan to have a baby, the first and third part of the equation are fallacies. All women do not have babies. Some women prefer not to for a variety of reasons, and still others are medically incapable of having a child. The only valid part of the statement is that *only* women can have babies. No male has ever successfully done the job of childbirth.

Okay, I can hear you. There was a news story not long ago in which it was claimed that a male did have a baby. This is true to a point. The fact of the matter is, though, that unless you listened carefully to that news story and made sense of the actual relevant material contained within it, you did not filter the information correctly.

76

The male in question had at one time been a female. Surgery had altered the appearance of his sex, but he/she had opted not to have his/her female reproductive system removed, as he and his/her partner desired a child. He made the decision to have a child after most of his anatomy had been changed from one sex to the other. He did not complete the surgeries for this purpose alone. As such, yes, a male had a baby. A male that had been born a female had a baby.

I can guarantee you with relative certainty that no other male, having been born a male, can deliver a child and experience pregnancy. Women are the only creatures who do this.

Keep in mind that all information is told from a particular perspective. In other words, you may be hearing only one angle that is but a part of a whole. You must learn to reason and think critically about things you hear or see in order to determine if any of the information is relevant to you or if it is worth remembering for your purposes.

Consider this if you will: I used to work in technology. I needed to know of new developments in that area and how to best use them to my advantage. I would probably take more interest in that than I would in what new perfume is on the market. The reason I say probably is that the perfume may become important to me if my wife decides she wants the latest scent to add to her collection. Unless my wife does this, however, I will dismiss the smell and retain the technologically advanced information as being the relevant source to remember. In this way, I have filtered out that which will not assist me in gaining success.

A writer will have different items of importance to help them reach their goals. Much of what a writer may consider to be important information will seem trivial to others. It is necessary to understand, observe, and then create viable worlds from the emotions and behaviors of others. A writer won't find information in the facts so much as in the emotions. The imagination will fill in the gaps to the actual event that created the emotion or behavior, and the writer will draw upon personal experience for the rest of the story, so to speak.

For example, a writer sees a young woman in tears. A young child clings to her leg. A man not much older than the young woman gives her a quick kiss and walks away. Now, if the writer had been paying attention to the conversation involved in this situation, she might have learned that the young man had been her brother and was leaving for a tour of duty in the armed forces overseas.

The imagination in the writer will take over, and a completely different story may emerge. The writer might decide that the scenario meant the young man had been her husband and was leaving his wife and child alone on a dreary winter day without the means to survive financially. The child is crying and clinging to his mother in fear of the new and strange circumstances that have befallen him. The mother is crying for the lost love she thought she had in her now-estranged husband. They may be tears of bitter abandonment or memories of happier times as she sets her mind to making her new circumstances work in her favor. In the end, the writer may have her overcoming every obstacle in her path, allowing a stumble now and then for credibility, and reuniting the young mother with her now more mature husband who is regretful. The writer may also have the young mother growing past the man who couldn't stand beside her and developing into an inspiration to others in similar situations.

As you can see, the filtering of information has to be based upon that information that you need for your purposes. In order to filter properly, you must have an idea of what your purpose is. Filtering without that much foresight will result in a disaster. You must responsibly decide what is important, and then retain that which supports your goals and desires on your journey to success. It will differ from person to person, and it is based upon the perception of self and the perception of the world in which we live.

In the process of learning to filter out that which you don't need, you will have less clutter on your way to discovering your successful path. Once you have learned to filter, you will find that the speed at which you are able to reach success will increase.

Use our workbook to help you with your overall path at *www. NaturalSuccessPrinciples.com/workbook.*

Chapter Twenty-One

Imagine Your Incredible Start From Just Two Cells

When you search for a solution to a problem, consider the possibility that the simple solution may be the most viable and best solution to your problem. This is true even with the most complex of situations.

"Life's problems wouldn't be called 'hurdles' if there wasn't a way to get over them."

—Anonymous

Jonna had a feeding tube during her stay in the NICU. Keep in mind that children who are born prematurely have a difficult time with reflux, as the tube keeps the stomach in a constant open state. There is a muscle that contracts and closes the stomach while food digests. It opens and closes as food is eaten to allow entry into the stomach and to keep the stomach acids in the stomach. In premature children, this muscle does not work as it should.

Jonna didn't escape this common difficulty of prematurity. She had reflux. If she was tipped, turned, or moved into different positions after a feeding and before the digestion of her food had been completed, she threw up. This created an obstacle to her gaining weight, which created the need for the feeding tube.

Now she had the essential feeding tube holding open the spout that kept her food in, so in my mind, the tube necessitated the need for a tube. Remove the tube, let the stomach sphincter heal and close, and the tube is no longer needed. Simple, huh? Well, after every feeding that I did, I then held her upright for forty-five minutes to an hour (yes, my arms hurt, but so what?) and this kept her food in so that it has time to pass to the intestines.

I asked the doctor if we could remove the tube so that I could hold her upright until the formula she had taken had been digested and was beyond the confines of her stomach. He agreed with a condition. If she lost weight for three days or more, the feeding tube would be put back in place, and I could not continue holding her upright to avoid the reflux that came otherwise.

The first day I was allowed to do this, Jonna lost weight. On the second day, she lost weight. When the third day came around, she remained at the same weight. I was granted a one-day stay due to this same weight. On the fourth day, Jonna gained weight. My simple solution had corrected a very complex problem for her. I can't tell you how many conversations me and my little girl had through this three-day test.

This is true for most situations and circumstances in life. We often search only for the most advanced or most difficult fix to our problems and overlook the simple ones. In so doing, we create more difficulties for ourselves.

If, for example, you are having some financial difficulty, you may jump immediately to the conclusion that the only solution is to increase the number of hours you work by securing a second job. Before that jump in logical order, however, you may want to consider a few more options.

Did you go through your finances to see where money wasn't being spent to the best advantage? If not, look. You might be surprised to find that by ridding yourself of items that do not give you a fair return on your investment you might eliminate all of your financial problems at the moment.

Have you investigated the possibility that your education is the root cause of your financial difficulty? Maybe you only need to upgrade that associate's degree to a bachelor's degree, which will command more money on your paycheck. Wouldn't it be more beneficial to your goals to fix your problem simply by getting an education rather than placing a thin and transparent band-aid over it, which is what a second job may be?

If you are seeking to use your Natural Principles, you may determine that your financial insecurity at the moment is the catalyst you need for change and begin to apply those principles to overcome your difficulty.

Another aspect of finding solutions is to try several different angles. For Jonna, we tried the feeding tube. That worked. As she progressed, we tried feeding orally. That took a while, but it did work. Then we tried holding her upright so she could digest that food without much reflux. That worked.

Problems may not have only one solution. You must decide if your problem or difficulty requires more than one solution. Perhaps a combination of tactics done simultaneously would benefit you the most. Maybe the best route is similar to what Jonna experienced where the solution came in the form of steps that documented her progress.

In the financial example, perhaps you need to consider a combination of examining your expenses for waste or unnecessary expenses, working a part-time job on the weekends to increase your payroll immediately, and taking classes at the college in the evening to increase future earning potential.

Whatever your decision in your set of circumstances, keep in mind that there are consequences to your actions. Not all consequences are negative. The consequence for making a right decision is success. That is what you want. Be committed to your decisions so that you may reap the benefits without stumbling off course from the Natural Success Principles you are unlocking within yourself.

If you want to succeed, you will. Already you have enough information from the previous chapters. If you are following them, you will find your situation improving. As you continue to seek the rest of the principles found in yourself before you were born and apply them to what you are already doing, your rate of success will increase.

I want to remind you that we are not defining success in dollar amounts, as success is different for everyone. Success is reached only when your definition of it is fulfilled. However, you may find that your definition will expand and grow with you.

In the beginning of this book, perhaps your idea of success was paying your monthly bills without needing to ask your mom or dad for a little help. You may have already reached that goal during the course of applying what you are learning to your life. If so, you might find that you are beginning to refine your definition of success. It may now be to not only pay your bills without assistance, but also to begin a savings account with twenty-five dollars a week deposited into it.

If this is the case for you and you've found that your definition is growing a bit, then congratulations. You have discovered that not only can success come at the moment, but that it can include future goals as well. As you grow in your success, you will find your self-esteem and confidence level rise as well.

I would suggest that you write down your beginning idea of success and then write down each change to that definition as it occurs to you. It will be a great way for you to physically see what your mind already knows. You deserve success and therefore will succeed.

Use our workbook to help you with your decisions at *www. NaturalSuccessPrinciples.com/workbook.*

Chapter Twenty-Two

"The Price of Greatness is Responsibility"

—Winston Churchill

"In every child who is born under no matter what circumstances and of no matter what parents, the potentiality of the human race is born again, and in him, too, once more, and each of us, our terrific responsibility toward human life; toward the utmost idea of goodness, of the horror of terrorism, and of God."
 —James Agee (1909-1955), *Let Us Now Praise Famous Men*

Let's talk about responsibility. You must take responsibility for your set of circumstances and the solution to those circumstances. No one else will care as much about your situation as you will. No one else will become as involved as you will be in your own situation. Therefore, take charge of that situation and make it the best it can be for you.

In no way is what I am about to say a negative reflection on the doctors and nurses who took care of Jonna. They were wonderful, caring people who had the expertise to care for my daughter when my wife and I couldn't because of Jonna's condition of prematurity.

Without them, I would not be able to write this book or any other, because my little angel wouldn't be here.

That being said, here goes: I took charge when I requested to hold Jonna upright for an hour or so after each feeding to help eliminate the problems caused by reflux. I was there for five feedings. She had four more feedings overnight. In her overnight feedings, Jonna was not held upright for an hour or so afterward. She regurgitated those feedings but held down the ones I was holding her after.

It wasn't that the doctors or nurses didn't care and wouldn't hold Jonna in the correct position for her to digest her food properly without losing as much as she ate in each bottle. They didn't have the time. Jonna wasn't the only baby in the NICU. There were many such babies. There was no time to hold each one for the right time span after feeding by the staff. Quite simply, they did the best they could but could not provide each baby with her own nursing staff and doctors. The babies had to share, and that meant they could not take the time to hold her upright after a feeding.

I took charge and did it. Why? Jonna was and is my child, my responsibility. I took the time because I was her father. I had a definite interest in her situation, as her situation was my situation. I could care more about her and about my circumstances than any of the nurses and doctors. I took responsibility for part of Jonna's care because it was what was best for Jonna, me, and my wife.

If you have a baby in the hospital, you must make time to be with that child. I'm not uncaring and do realize that some parents could not have financially afforded the time that I spent with Jonna. Trust me, we learned to squeeze a nickel, and Taco Bell knows it. Maybe there are other children at home to consider, or the parents are too sick to be in the NICU and would pose a threat to the babies. There are circumstances that prevent spending the entire time with your baby at times in the NICU, no matter how much you may want to be there. But you should take the initiative and try. You should work out a regular schedule to be there. You should take responsibility, because your child needs you to visit them. Love does as much, if not more, for these infants as technology and medicine. Be there, take charge, pick up the reigns, and accept the responsibility for the new life you helped to create.

In all aspects of your life, you must take responsibility for what is happening. If you don't, you become a victim of circumstance instead of a leader of change. You must be your own advocate. You must be the voice of control, and you must take responsibility, not only for the current situation, but for the actions taken in that set of circumstances that bring about positive change.

"Character—the willingness to accept responsibility for one's own life—is the source from which self respect springs."
—Joan Didion (1934-), *Slouching Towards Bethlehem*

You cannot sit passively by and hope that someone will come along and save you. If you need saving, dig deep within yourself, use this book and all of its other facets, and save yourself. You really are the only one who cares enough about you and your family to pull it off. The rest of the world is trying to do it for their families. If, and that is a big if, someone does manage to find the time to bail you out, they might come to your aid. The question is, are you willing to sacrifice your success on the prayer that someone else will do it for you? Take control. Accept your own responsibility. Make your own change.

Now I am about to say something very profound. No one—not your parents, not government, not neighbors—no one can help you succeed if you do not take the responsibility to help yourself.

We go into this in great detail in a later chapter, because this is and will continue to be the most important lesson learned.

Use our workbook to help you with your responsibilities at *www. NaturalSuccessPrinciples.com/workbook*.

Chapter Twenty-Three

"Life Grants Nothing to Mortals Without Hard Work"
—Horace

Now that you know it is your responsibility to care for your own set of circumstances and to exit the role of the victim once and for all, let's discuss working in the sense of what you do for a living. Yes, I am sure that everyone must work in some capacity. Some types of employment are more lucrative than others, and that is in direct correlation to the skill level needed to perform the job.

However, that doesn't change a fundamental fact of life that will determine your attitude toward your job. If you are going to do it, do it well. It does not matter what "it" is! There is no excuse for half-jobs in the workplace. If it is worth putting effort forth for, then you should make that effort count. When you neglect this simple concept, you waste time. Time is too precious to waste. It cannot be refilled.

It is not my intent to make you feel as if you must have a professional job in order to have one that matters. Every single type of work is needed in order to have our society continue to run smoothly. From maids and housekeepers to the President of the United States, there is no unimportant job to have. Each profession within each level of skilled and unskilled work has a place and is needed.

Nonetheless, if you flip burgers at the local fast food restaurant, then you should take pride in doing your job. There are cartoon characters that do this. SpongeBob SquarePants is but one of them. He makes Krabby Patties at a restaurant under the sea, but he has a great pride in his work. He is proud to be a short order cook of Krabby Patties and is proud of his ability to be the best fry cook under the sea.

"Work will win when wishy washy wishing won't."
—Thomas S. Monson (1927-)

The army had a slogan: Be all you can be. They had that because they wanted soldiers in their ranks who have pride in the work of protecting our country. They want the soldiers who care about what they are doing and believe in what they are doing.

Computer programmers need to care about the software they are creating, what it does, and how it is used. Waitresses need to care about the service a patron in a restaurant receives. Maids need to care about how clean a room is when they are finished with it. Work like you don't need the money. It will change the way you perform your tasks.

"Work while you have the light. You are responsible for the talent that has been entrusted to you."
—Henri-Frédéric Amiel (1821-1881)

If you care about your work, you will find ways to excel at the task before you. You may even discover a better and more efficient method of doing your job. That's the spirit that breeds pride and success at work while reducing stress at the same time. It also allows you to feel a sense of accomplishment about the work you perform. All of these things combined enhance your ability to harness the power of your own natural success.

If you are proud of what you do, there is a sense of accomplishment that you are a contributing member of a valuable service, and you should be proud. I am very proud of my accomplishments. Even though some of what I have done is not seen publically, as I am proud of my private accomplishments as well, I find that when I can appreciate the value of my work, I am a happier and more successful man.

"Think enthusiastically about everything; but especially about your job. If you do, you'll put a touch of glory in your life. If you love your job with enthusiasm, you'll shake it to pieces. You'll love it into greatness."

—Norman Vincent Peale (1898-1993)

I know of a woman who never worked in the public venue. She never held a job, nor did she ever earn a dime. She did, however, make a wonderful contribution to society that she had great pride in. She raised her family. She reared her children with love and kindness and a firm hand. She cared for them and worried over them. She made one of the greatest accomplishments of life her goal, her measure of success.

She never complained of cooking over a pot bellied wood stove or of the canning she did with fruits and vegetables she grew herself. The clothes she sewed deep in the hours of the night until her fingers bled were priceless and well-made. When one of her children received such a gift from her, their reaction was that of receiving their own pot of gold at the end of the rainbow.

When she passed, she knew she hadn't wasted her time by investing it unwisely in her children. She knew she had given the world several contributing members of society, and she was proud of what she had done with her life. She passed on to them her strong work ethic and her strong sense of honesty and integrity.

Would her children have felt that what their mother did was so special if she had not been proud of her job? She had the most important job in the world: Raising children. She didn't get a fat paycheck for her work, as no amount of money could have paid her an adequate salary for all she did in a day; but because she was proud of her job, others were proud of her.

If you are proud and feel that sense of accomplishment in whatever you do in your life, others will feel it too. If you're a writer, then you should feel pleased with the words you've written upon a page. If you are a mother who works to take care of your home and family and don't have an outside job, you should feel the same amount of accomplishment as the President of the United States feels when elected. Your work is just as important and just as appreciated by others.

It snowballs. I know pride cometh before the fall, but not this type of pride. When you feel you are better than everyone else, the adage that delegates pride into a sinful and undesirable attribute may be true. However, when pride is used to motivate and reach a sense of accomplishment in a job well done, I don't think you are in danger of great strife heading your way.

You will never have to feel sorry for doing a job well done. Also, you should not think less of yourself when you see others not working. Do not fall prey to the herd mentality. Do not feel guilty for being you and being successful.

"The pride of the peacock is the glory of God."
—William Blake (1757-1827)

I do think that such pride unleashes the confidence that is necessary to unlock the success within you. Go ahead and put in the key of pride. Turn it in the lock and let your success shine through.

Use our workbook to list your accomplishments at *www.NaturalSuccessPrinciples.com/workbook*.

Chapter Twenty-Four

Bulldog It (Tenacity)

When you set your goals of success, you must make sure that you are clear in your definition of where you want to be when you've reached the end of your journey to success before you take on another journey to success. You may find that your path will change in order to overcome the obstacles in your path, but you must remain focused on the end result.

"Man is a goal seeking animal. His life only has meaning if he is reaching out and striving for his goals."

—Aristotle (384-322 BC)

When Jonna was in the NICU, our goal was to take our baby home. I could see her in her own crib, hear her laughing as we played in the living room, and feel her snuggled against me as we watched the football game. Never did I lose sight of the goal to take Jonna home. For 130 days, and more if you count all of the time since the pregnancy began up until Jonna's birth, I did the same thing, saw the same thing, and had the same goal.

It was difficult at times, especially when we rounded a corner and found a solid wall of granite standing in our way. We found ways of going over, under, around, and through every single thing that happened along the way because the goal was clear. Jonna would go home no matter what we had to do to make that happen for her. We would have our child free of tubes and needles and asleep in her own crib in the nursery that awaited her at our house. Our friends and family would visit her without doctors and nurses everywhere. My wife and I would be parents in a normal setting and without the stress of the hospital as our daily backdrop. We knew this because Jonna would come home.

Each time we took a step backward, tripped, or stumbled, we focused on the goal of getting her home. We were persistent in our efforts to see our goal realized and would visualize no other possible outcome.

That is what you must be when you set a goal: Persistent. You cannot give up just because something gets in your way. If you quit, then your goal disappears and becomes unreachable. You, at that point, have decided on a new definition of success, and that definition is clouded with failure.

You avoid this by setting clear goals and following through with the tenacity of a bulldog. You keep focused and continue to persist even when the odds are stacked against you. Nothing in your actions should indicate anything but the absolute certainty that you will get around the necessary obstacles in your path any way you can to reach your final goal.

When you remain persistent in your efforts and focused on your goals, then the Natural Success Principles that you have been learning will do the rest. You will find a way to succeed no matter how bleak the situation nor how dire the circumstances.

"A goal is a dream with a deadline."

—Napoleon Hill (1883-1970)

If your goal is to be financially stable in a period of five years and you are starting from a situation in which you can barely make your bills currently, then stay focused on that goal. Do whatever you can to see it through. This may mean going to school while you work a full-time job and raise the kids.

Your marital status doesn't have a thing to do with your chances of reaching your goals. There are single mothers out there who have taken themselves and their children from poor to wealthy within years by working for their goals. These women haven't wavered in their efforts to reach what they considered success and the accumulation of their goals. They realized their dreams by squashing anything that got in their way.

If you need a visual of this, you must watch *The Pursuit of Happyness*. The trials of the man in the movie never once stopped him from reaching his goal of success. He went through some horrendous experiences, but he found a way to do it all.

We went through rough periods with Jonna. She was given only a 30 percent chance of survival because of her gestational age of twenty-five weeks at birth. We were told that we could lose her, that many premature babies didn't make it. We were prepared by the doctors for the worst, but we only believed in our goal: Taking Jonna home. We were determined, persistent, and unwavering in our pursuit of that goal.

That is the type of tenacity that comes from unlocking the Natural Success Principles within you. We wanted a particular and clear result. We went after it as if that were the only possible scenario as an end result. We tapped into that principle to reach our goal and success.

"Nothing in the world can take the place of Persistence. Talent will not; nothing is more common than unsuccessful men with talent. Genius will not; unrewarded genius is almost a proverb. Education will not; the world is full of educated derelicts. Persistence and determination alone are omnipotent. The slogan 'Press On' has solved and always will solve the problems of the human race."

—Calvin Coolidge (1872-1933)

Yes, I realize that I had experienced success prior to Jonna's birth, but it was the success that I felt at getting to take our baby home that made me feel as if I had accomplished the most I could on this earth. The releasing of my natural success within me made the victory of her journey the sweetest and most precious of accomplishments I have ever had or will have again. This is also the reason for everything I am now. I must share what I learned to grow past the knowledge I gained.

Find your reason for being tenacious and persistent in your pursuit of success through the natural success process, and you will discover the joy that it brings. It really is incomparable.

Use our workbook to help you with your overall goals at *www.NaturalSuccessPrinciples.com/workbook.*

Chapter Twenty-Five

Fear Cannot Live in Preparedness

When Jonna was in the NICU, we had doctors and nurses who handled any emergency that came up with her. If she stopped breathing, they were right there with the respirator to get her going again. If she developed a condition that required surgery, they stood at the ready. They were prepared for any situation of any magnitude at any hour of the day or night.

When we began seeing how close we were to realizing our goal of taking Jonna home, we began to take classes in infant CPR. We learned everything we could about every possible emergency that we could possibly face. We didn't think of it as a probability of happening, but we did think of it as a preparation for the unknown.

"It seems to me that people have vast potential. Most people can do extraordinary things if they have the confidence or take the risks. Yet most people don't. They sit in front of the telly and treat life as if it goes on forever."

—Philip Adams (1939-)

There was no fear of taking her home because of that preparedness that we had taken the time to learn. In doing so, we erased any crack in our thoughts through which negativity could enter. We never thought of what could happen, but instead continued to see our little Jonna Lil running amuck in our home, making messes as she giggled gleefully. That's what we saw. We were ready.

In any situation that arises and in all changes that life brings in its wake, there is an element of fear. You can erase that fear by employing the Natural Success Principles inside you. It's how my wife and I overcame the fear that so many thought we should have had as we were taking our premature daughter home without the convenience of a doctor or nurse at our sides.

By preparing for the possibilities, we erased the fears of what happens "if." There are a lot of "what ifs." What if she stops breathing? What if she stops eating? What if she gets a cold? What if she gets a fever? Quite frankly, there are too many "what ifs" to mention in their entirety.

Instead of focusing on those factors, we chose to keep up our own persistence in the goal we had set, we learned, and we became prepared. We armed ourselves with knowledge. And we discovered what we already knew: We could do this.

> "Confidence is courage at ease."
> —Daniel Maher (1881-1916)

Knowing you can do something takes a great deal of self-esteem. Through the unleashing of Natural Success Principles, you will develop a healthy dose of self-esteem that will see you through the hardest of circumstances. I have always been blessed with more than my fair share of self-esteem. There isn't anything I don't think I can do. Because I don't know I can't succeed, I do succeed. If asked, I will tell you that I can do anything you ask me to do.

When I started writing this book and my previous book to document Jonna's journey and the natural success that I learned from her, I didn't know I couldn't. If you had told me it was impossibile, I would have taken that as a challenge and proved you wrong. Some mistake the confidence I have in myself for arrogance, but it isn't. I simply choose to utilize every aspect of the lessons that Jonna taught me and use them to my advantage, as they were meant to be used.

You can make the same choice in your life. There is no reason at all that you cannot meet your dreams head-on when you decide you would like to do something. You may have to employ help, prioritize, and visualize, but you can do it. That is the wonder of your true being. You have limitless potential from before you were born to this very moment. Everyone can do it once they learn how to do it.

I didn't know how to do infant CPR before the classes I took to ensure that I was prepared to bring Jonna home. I listened, I learned, and I owned the knowledge I gained to benefit me and my family.

That is also something that you must realize. It isn't enough to simply find the information you seek. You must listen to it, absorb it, and allow it to become a part of you on your quest to reach your goal. I could have taken the course in infant CPR and paid no attention. I could have decided to learn just the minimum. I could have given the class half my effort. I didn't. I wanted it to bring me the most advantageous benefits. I wanted to make sure I knew what had to be done and could do it without hesitation should the need arise. I wanted to own every morsel of knowledge that was placed upon my plate and savor it so I would know the flavor anywhere should I have need of it again.

Preparedness is a key to any success. Think about it. Would you fill the tires of your car after you drove the car a hundred miles? Of course not. You would have made sure you had air in your tires, a spare in your trunk, a lug wrench, and a jack before you put the key in the ignition and started the engine. If you will take that much care for your car, you should take it for every aspect of your life. Prepare for every moment you can and reap the benefits of making molehills of mountains because of that preparedness.

As you learn to harness your success, own the knowledge you gain, constantly test and seek growth, prepare for the bend around the corner, and believe you will succeed. As success comes to you, expect nothing less. Persist in your pursuit of success as you develop and evolve your definition of success. Believe you can when everyone else swears you can't. Success is waiting for you to claim it. You must allow it to happen to you.

Use our workbook to help you with your preparation at *www. NaturalSuccessPrinciples.com/workbook*.

Chapter Twenty-Six

Mirror, Mirror on the Wall, Why Ask You?

Self-esteem is one of the most important attributes you can have that will catapult you to success within the definitions of natural success. I don't mean that you should think yourself some sort of God on the planet earth that should be listened to no matter how insane your ideas. Self-esteem does give confidence that you can do more than you may have thought in the past, but it doesn't transcend some basic laws of physics.

> "Low self-esteem is like driving through life with your hand-brake on."
> —Maxwell Maltz (1899-1975)

When there is something to be done, you must believe you can do it. If you delegate the task to another, you can't even explain to someone else how to manage it and make it work if you don't believe you can do it. Put simply, if you don't believe you can, you probably can't.

Self-esteem is the perception you have of yourself. Just as you can't really love another person until you can love yourself, you can't succeed in gaining a high level of success if you don't believe in yourself. Your mantra must be *I can do it, I can do it, and I can do it.* It doesn't matter the complexity of the task at hand. You must—and I really can't stress this enough—believe you can do anything that comes up in life.

Many people see computer code and think, "Oh no, I can't read that! I can't learn to do that!" Once they give in to that thought, they no longer have the ability to do it. Yet computer languages aren't difficult to learn. What makes them seem that way is the attitude that comes with them.

In school, girls are said to be worse at math than boys. This simply isn't true. I know many women who excel in mathematics. Gender doesn't stop you from becoming great in any area—you stop yourself with a low image of your own abilities.

Natural success brings that back into focus by giving you the confidence you need to build up your self-esteem to succeed even when the area in question isn't your chosen area of expertise. It is an attitude, a belief in your ability to learn anything that you don't already know, and a sense of pride in that ability that patches self-esteem and creates greatness where normalcy stood before.

All of the psychologists out there constantly bombard us with reasons why self-esteem is a major issue in school-age children. They cite teasing as self-esteem's destroyer. In reality, self-esteem's destroyer is the person who has low self-esteem. It can't be teasing, or no one would have a sense of self that was positive in nature.

Every school-aged child in America (and probably the world) has withstood some teasing. This is simply the way our society works. This is how human nature works. We tease and try to show ourselves in a good light. The difference between the child who learns to feel poorly about himself and the one who learns to see himself as a success is in the attitude. One believes the teasing, and the other chooses to filter out that information and discard it for what it is: Extra garbage he doesn't need.

I have always had high self-esteem. Now I know why. Many of the principles of Natural Success were in place and active, but not enough of them were in place to complete the picture before Jonna pointed them out. They were integral parts of my personality and the personalities of a faction of the population that has a good self-image. Jonna taught me to use them to the best of my advantage, but they were in place upon my birth.

You need to develop your self-esteem and refuse to allow the image of yourself to stand in your way of success. Think of yourself as valuable, and you will be. It will become apparent to everyone who meets you as well. You will exude the confidence you need to find the path to your goals, regardless of the obstacles you may face.

You can't let anyone, not even yourself, stand in your way. You must learn to believe in the goals you have set and practice the principles of Natural Success you have learned without fail. You can and will succeed if you do. If not, then you will have no one to blame but yourself. It's your life. Take charge of it and face the music of your decisions with it, both good and bad.

Use our workbook to help you with your self-esteem at *www. NaturalSuccessPrinciples.com/workbook.*

Chapter Twenty-Seven

Your Mind Has Learned Failure

Failure is a learned behavior that creates another form of success: Learned success. Learned success is not the same as natural success, but it does have a place in this book, as most people are more familiar with learned success.

When Jonna was in the NICU, the only definition of success she knew was her Natural Success Principles. This continued as she grew until she passed the toddler stage. Up until that point, Jonna had no concept of a different kind of success. She only knew what was already inside of her. She drew off of it and depended upon the natural principles that she had at her disposal.

Like any child, she began to learn by the third year of her life that there was a concept called "wrong." With the introduction of this new concept, Jonna began to do as we all do. She began to hide her Natural Success Principles in exchange for success defined by right and wrong. This led to her first understandings of learned success.

If Jonna did right by the standards of an outside source of authority, such as me or her mother, she learned to accept that as success in achieving good behavior. If she did wrong, she learned the emotions that go along with failure. Eventually she began to test the limits of what was on each side of the fence. Those behaviors and actions that didn't meet with approval and therefore were deemed wrong became the ones that she avoided. Those actions and behaviors that were met with approval and were considered right, Jonna strove to continue.

Every day, as her understanding of these basic concepts grows, she applies what she has learned to newly learned or attempted skills. When she fails at a new skill, she discovers that she has done it wrong, which she cannot separate from *incorrect*. If I allowed her to stop the new skill based upon her understanding of wrong and the emergence of failure, she would not attempt it a second time. Instead, I must make her learn to try the skill again and again until she can do it correctly (or *right*) in her way of viewing things.

This begins the concepts of success according to what society believes success to be. We learn from an early age that successful people have large bank accounts, drive fancy cars, and travel extensively at whim. We are also taught that many of them work hard for their success and that is used to instill a strong work ethic within us.

We are also told that some people who are seen as successful do not work for their success but inherit it. There is a lessening of respect in our view of those who have been handed success without the sweat that should have been poured into achieving that goal. There is also something strange going on in the country that seems to be punishment for being successful. You are to feel guilty that your hard work paid off and that you are now able to live from the fruits of your labor. This is simply someone who has covered their own Natural Success Principles and chooses to tear down others rather than build themselves up. This is a sad commentary on today's society. It must be overcome.

This gives us our first taste of what society expects of us as productive members within its confines. What it doesn't make clear to us is that *wrong, right, correct*, and *incorrect* all have very different meanings and connotations. Failure to do a task or perform a skill accurately the first time it is attempted is not wrong. It is incorrect, but it isn't wrong. Doing a task correctly or displaying a skill correctly doesn't make it right.

Now, that should be confusing to some. Let me explain. The dexterity in hand movement is a necessary skill. However, if the skill is displayed by showing vulgar signs, the correct display of dexterity isn't a right action to take. Therefore, although dexterity is displayed correctly, in this case it would fall under the *wrong* category in sorting out the failure to display a skill in an acceptable manner. In effect, the message sent is a learned failure because the goal is to learn to conduct yourself in an acceptable way within society's definitions of right and wrong. Flipping someone off isn't a success by society's measure no matter how well it displays a skill in dexterity, which is needed in life.

By the same token, when we learn a skill that is acceptable and considered a thing of value that will assist us in our quest for success, we repeat that skill and build upon it. Displaying dexterity by learning to use a keyboard on a computer to type code or words upon a page is seen not only as a successful display of the skill and is therefore considered *right* in the eyes of society, it also displays the skill correctly.

Now, I hear those of you who are whispering that I haven't shown you how *incorrect* can be *right*. Let's do that now. Jonna sits down to write a letter to her grandparents thanking them for the birthday gift she received. In that letter, she makes letters backwards, misspells words, and uses some words for purposes that were never intended, giving them new meanings as she doesn't know their correct meanings yet. While her letter is written incorrectly and has bad form, her intent of action by thanking them for their generosity to her is a right action. In this case, her very incorrectly written letter is an acceptable use of the skill that allows her to display gratitude to another. It highlights the manners she is being taught that are needed to maneuver in today's society.

All the while, through this process of learning what success is and what it means to society, Jonna is burying the very Natural Success Principles that she had always displayed without attempting to fit into the world she must enter. These success principles will lie hidden within her until she finds the catalyst to revisit them during the course of her life.

Still, it is important to remember that because society's definition of success is learned, trying must occur in order to gain proficiency in those things that are needed. This is why I insist that Jonna keep trying, even when she perceives herself to have failed and done something wrong. She must learn not to quit, just as she has started to learn success instead of relying on her natural abilities.

You must do this as well. You must be able to distinguish between learned success and natural success in order to reach the depths of your buried Natural Success Principles and reach your goals in life. Without the ability to tell the difference, necessary things that you need from your Natural Success Principles may be left buried during the time it takes you to realize it.

Learn to try. Learn to do so even when you fail. True failure only occurs when you no longer try to learn and continue to grow in the knowledge you gain on a daily basis. This is a key to realizing the natural success within you. It is one of the things that allows you to use your natural success and to believe in your ability to succeed when the odds seem to be insurmountable in nature. Recognize that which is already in you, and determine for yourself how much of society's definition of success you intend to take for your own. You may choose to throw out society's definition altogether, but you will have a more clear view of the goals you set for yourself and the methods you need to use to reach them.

Use our workbook to help you with your Natural Success Principles at *www.NaturalSuccessPrinciples.com/workbook*.

Chapter Twenty-Eight

Have A Parade! Pronounce Yourself To New Heights.

Now that you realize that there is a separate type of success and that failure is learned, it's time to examine how we come to fail when it is an undesired result. Could it be that the fear of succeeding within society's definition of success drives a need to tip the scales onto what is perceived as failure in order to avoid the changes that success would bring in your life? Are you attempting to remain within the comfort zone that you have become accustomed to throughout your life? Did you learn that a certain amount of failure was not only acceptable, but expected?

Fear of success is very real. Some people feel that the changes success would bring to their life would change their basic personality, causing them to become something they don't want to be. In truth, that type of change only occurs because of choices made at the time that success enters one's life. Also note that, as I have said before, success does not have to mean financial success. That is society's definition.

"Your success depends mainly upon what you think of yourself and whether you believe in yourself."
—William J. H. Boetcker (1873-1962)

My definition of success during the time that Jonna was in NICU was not financial. I wanted the success of bringing my daughter home and raising a family just as everyone I knew did with their children and wives. No amount of money was going to make that happen. Slipping the doctor a couple thousand wouldn't make him release her from the hospital before she was ready to be released. Again, money did help her in paying for the costs of medical care for a premature child, but it would not give me my definition of success in reality. Only time would do that—time and effort to learn how to make it happen and then pursuing the goal.

When you are deciding if you are worried about the changes in you as a person that will occur as a byproduct of success, consider the definition that you have set in place of success. Is it the same as society's? Would you really make the choice to change in undesirable ways when you employ your success principles, and can you justify continuing to harbor failure in exchange for your own happiness? I think in the end, you will find that the joy brought to you by the change of success in realizing your goals using your Natural Success Principles will exude to those around you. The changes will be more beneficial than harmful and will create a desire in you to continue to use natural success over learned success.

If you are failing to reach outside of a personal comfort zone, then examine your idea of success. Perhaps you have already reached the goals you see for yourself in life at this time. Maybe you feel some obligation to stay where you are and in the same situations. But if you don't like where your life has ended up at this point, then man or woman up and change it. No one else can change it for you, and no one else will. If you don't get off your rump and take charge of your situation, then you deserve to be where you are. Just don't whine to the rest of us who choose to succeed. When you're good and ready, you'll make the effort to take responsibility and change your circumstance. Once you do, you will find success a much sweeter option than what you have known before.

If you are one of those who somehow got a mixed message on failure being acceptable and desirable but only in certain quantities, then you will need to change your viewpoint. You must learn to believe that failure is not an option under any circumstances. It isn't okay to fail no matter what the writing on the wall may be telling you. Who wrote the stuff on that wall anyway? You did. That means you can change what's there. You can make the effort to abolish failure from your acceptable outcomes of your circumstances.

No matter the reason for failing at will, there is something that can help you overcome the obstacle of failure: Affirmation. Find it. Use it. Learn to believe it. Be persistent in your pursuit of affirmations. Change with the affirmations and start on the path that will end in the realization of your dreams.

By now you should have realized that I can hear you reading. I didn't say a word about the kind of boring and rather obnoxious affirmations that claim you are the lost God of the Planet and you are now found. Those are not only annoying, but they are harmful in the fact that they only give you a delusion.

When I speak of affirmation, I mean the sort that teaches you to see fundamental truths in your Natural Success Principles. You do deserve success. You can achieve success. You will find your way to the goals you have set despite the obstacles. There is nothing you can't learn to do. You really can find your own pot of gold at the end of a rainbow. Granted, it may be a type of gold that only you recognize as such, but it is your pot anyway.

Also, I'm not talking about literal gold here. Maybe your pot holds the designs for clothing that you would love to create but haven't reached yet. Perhaps it's a lawn that is cut so that it looks like a lush, emerald carpet, and maybe it's getting to take your child home to live after an extensive stay in NICU. These are pots filled with your dreams, your goals, and you get to them by believing you can succeed in obtaining them.

If you need to, and for many this does help, record your affirmations and listen to them in the car on the way to work. The more you affirm your right to succeed, the stronger the belief becomes within you. Maybe you could sing them in the shower. Write notes with your affirmations on them and stick them where you will see them often. All of these are good ways to constantly and consistently affirm your right to success to unlock in you the Natural Success Principles that make success happen on any level and to any degree that you wish it to happen. You are the only limit that is truly placed upon you. Locate the ways to affirm your success that work for you, and then realize your goals.

Use our workbook to help you with your affirmations at *www. NaturalSuccessPrinciples.com/workbook*.

Chapter Twenty-Nine

Failure Leads to Success—Yeah, I Said It

There is something you should know about failure. Although it isn't what you should aim for as an end result, it is necessary in order for success to be easy. Failure, used in the right manner, is the tool that allows us to learn and grow closer to success. Failure makes success easy by allowing us to take away lessons from something we have done that has failed and to apply those lessons to new endeavors and goals in our ever-changing quest of goals we set for ourselves.

"It is possible to fail in many ways. While to succeed is possible only in one way."

—Aristotle (384-322 BC)

I have had five businesses. I have lost five businesses. Guess what? Each time I failed at a business, I took the knowledge I gained through the attempt of that business and applied it to the next business. In return, none of my five businesses failed for the same reason. Instead, I have grown and know more now than when I first started trying to run a business. I have discovered the goals I have set for myself, and I keep trying. Failure to me has not meant throwing in the towel and quitting. Instead, it has brought positive aspects to my life because I learned from every single one of the failures I have had.

Some of you may think that it's not so bad to fail in business, but what about failing to produce a child that lives when that is the goal? It really is the same thing. There is a positive to be learned even if a child dies. If Jonna had died, it would not have been a failure to me. I still would have had the chance to meet the angel sent to earth for me. The memory of her, no matter how short, would have been a blessing to me.

Now, yes, it may seem easier to say than to actually have to deal with it, I know. Most things are, but the point I'm trying to make is that there is a positive to every single thing in your life. Jonna would have been a blessing even if she had died. She is a miracle and a glorious blessing because she lived. Still, she would have had a positive influence on my life either way. It is just that God saw fit to give me this angel instead of allowing me only a glimpse of her. She must have much more to teach me on this earth, and I am willing and ready to learn from her.

Your losses in life actually help to make life easier by balancing success and tempering egos to keep you functioning in a manner that allows you to continue to grow. Death balances your appreciation of life. The death of a business balances the importance you place on planning for the future. Both have a positive influence upon your life even when it may seem that the opposite is true.

Now, I'm not saying that the two types of loss mentioned have the same effect emotionally. They aren't even close. I am saying that any loss you suffer will make you stronger and make you grow in ways you didn't even know existed. The death of child is obviously tragic and devastating, while the loss of a business may only reach melancholy. Both experiences, though, will place you on a new level of learning that will make things in your life easier since you will be armed with even more knowledge than when you started.

I should also point out that I would not and do not wish anyone to lose their child. Remember, my daughter's heart stopped twice. I could not imagine to what degree of anguish I would have succumbed; so believe me when I say, I shall not ever wish for anyone to suffer the loss of a child. The emotional devastation is drastic, and rightly so. Still, it is better to have had the child to love, if only for a little while, than it would have been not to have known your child at all.

It is all about balance. Balance stabilizes you and causes you to become more even-tempered. It takes a lot to get me angry, and it should you, too. The reason is that perfect balance that life gives you through failures when attempting something new, and success when you master it.

Balance also occurs when you have a great deal to be thankful for in your life. Everyone does. If you don't think you have anything to be thankful for, then make a list. Write it down. Here is where that workbook you get for free comes in handy. There's the love of your family, your children, your parents, your spouse, and your friends. If you don't have any of those, then list the love of your pets, or your passions, or whatever it is that you are thankful for in your life.

If you really can't find even one positive in your life that you can list, then go make one. Do it right now. Put down this book and go to a local restaurant, coffee shop, grocery store, it doesn't matter. Ask someone there how they are, and then listen to their response. Really listen. If they have a problem that you can solve, do so. Make a difference. Make your own positive influences. Give the waitress a bigger tip than you normally would have on any other day. Tell the clerk how great they have made your day in the grocery store. It's that easy to make a positive difference in your life and in the lives of others.

If you are still sitting there saying that there is nothing positive in your life and you can't put this book down and go make one, then you're reading the wrong book in the first place. If that's the case, you don't need to listen to me at all. There isn't anything I can do for you. Don't come to my seminars. Don't enroll in my classes. Don't read any more of my books. For that matter, don't buy any more of my books or any other book. Don't even watch television. I also request that you not venture out into society, lest you leach your lowly thoughts on others. You are beyond any help at all from anyone.

Instead, sit at home and wallow in self-pity. You have nothing and never will. Until you make the decision to change and to find success, stay in your world of chosen failure and enjoy the pain and sadness it brings to you. You can't be helped until you are ready to help yourself. When you are, feel free to try again to locate your Natural Success Principles. Until then, you can remain a pitiful mar upon society's back.

If you fit the above description, you don't need our workbook at *www.NaturalSuccessPrinciples.com/workbook.*

Chapter Thirty

"Knowledge Speaks, but Wisdom Listens"
—Jimi Hendrix

Wisdom: It is the byproduct of all of the experiences you have had in your life. It is the well of knowledge from everything you have ever done. Wisdom is the accumulation of thoughts, emotions, and skills over time. It is the abyss of everything you have ever learned. It is also another major key to your success.

"Wisdom is your perspective on life, your sense of balance, your understanding of how the various parts and principles apply and relate to each other. It embraces judgment, discernment, comprehension. It is gestalt or oneness, and integrated wholeness."

—Stephen R. Covey (1932-)

You will acquire wisdom whether you want to or not. That being said, you might as well make a note of what you know and draw upon that for assistance in making decisions that affect your life. Make the right decisions, and you will reap success naturally. Make the wrong decisions, and you will follow a detour that leads away from your goals until you change that decision to make it right.

Wisdom is often referred to as common sense. Most people forget to use their stores of knowledge responsibly and are lacking in this trait to varying degrees. This can impede their ability to reach success as quickly as they should, since they will be backtracking often to rectify poor choices.

For example, let's suppose you have a friend named Mike. Mike has a history of having unexplained wrecks. He is the only person you know who has wrecked his car when his car was the only thing in sight for miles. There were no telephone poles, no ditches, no other cars. Nothing. Yet Mike still managed to total his car.

Mike gets a new car. He offers to take you for a spin to check out his new ride. You already know that Mike can't drive and that he obtained his license from a Cracker Jack box. If you get into the car with Mike and allow him to drive you somewhere, you are an idiot. You have displayed a complete lack of common sense or any traces of wisdom beyond common sense.

Instead, when Mike asks you to let him drive you around in his new wheels, you need to run in the other direction as fast as you can go. It is dangerous. You know this from his driving history. Don't be an idiot. Use the knowledge you have and save yourself. Trust me on this one: Mike will not save you. Mike will likely kill you, or at the very least, injure you during your ride with him. Do not go. That is the smart thing to do.

I hope you also see that Mike and his car are analogies for anyone with anything bad that you know in your life.

Wisdom leads to very good intuition. You know in your heart that you should not go to certain places at certain times. This can only lead to bad things. Use this wisdom and make better choices.

Experience that you learn throughout your life poses as a backdrop for what I like to call the wisdom chest within you. Just as common sense is to be used, so are all other forms of wisdom. Do not ignore the wisdom chest. It will enable you to make more informed and better decisions because you can draw upon past experiences to handle your current situation.

Let's say you go to work and find out that your boss has promoted someone else for a position you wanted. The person he has decided is a better candidate has worked for the company for less time than you have and has only half of your experience in the field. This makes you angry. You decide to tell your boss exactly what you think of him.

After you spend your five minutes of anger yelling obscenities at your boss, you somehow find yourself packing up your desk and going home. He has fired you for your outburst.

Now let's think about your wisdom chest. What should you put in there for future reference should this situation arise again? I will give you a few moments to decide, and then come back with your answers. Go ahead, think about it. Lay the book down and examine everything you should have learned from this scenario. Use our workbook to help you with your wisdom chest here at *www.NaturalSuccessPrinciples.com/workbook.*

Then when you have your answer, pick this book back up and read on.

If your answer is, "The nerve of my boss for passing me up on the promotion!" you are not using your wisdom chest wisely. Perhaps you should spend a day cleaning out that chest and replacing the crap you've collected with useful information.

If your answer describes the sense of satisfaction you felt at venting on your boss, then go immediately to the head of the welfare line. It is where you will spend most of your life. You will also need to clean out your wisdom chest and replace the crap with useful knowledge.

If you came up with the fact that you should not repeat the mistake of yelling obscenities at your boss, you may be on the right track. The reason I say you may be, and not that you are, is that your answer depends on whether the next thought had something to do with another form of communication to exact the same explosion of your opinion on your boss. If you thought about writing it down and giving it to your boss in a letter laced with poison, then you can go join the welfare line as well. Of course, you will not be at the head of that line, as you must first redecorate your living quarters to include steel bars and striped uniforms.

Now, if you decided that you shouldn't repeat the obscenities scene in any way and instead should simply accept his decision while you make positive changes in your life that will land you a better position in another company that will appreciate you, then you get a gold star. Don't repeat yelling at the boss. Bosses don't like it. They will fire you for this behavior. Instead of colorizing your language, improve yourself, and make positive changes in your own life.

Every day, your chest of wisdom should grow. However, don't fill the wisdom chest with crap that you can't use and that won't help you reach your goals. Just as you should be careful with your time, you should be careful with what you hold on to for use in future situations. Make each deposit in your chest of knowledge count. It will help you when you need it the most.

When you do have future situations arise, don't jump to your chest of wisdom with the intent of grabbing the first thing you come across as the answer to your current problem. Instead, sift through it. Look at each possible solution you know of, and try to see the benefits and the pitfalls of each one. Then choose the answer that bests fits the desired end result you wish to have. By doing it in this manner, you will be ensuring that your decisions will continue to move you forward toward your goals by way of the most direct route.

"Each time you deviate from the most direct route to your goals, you lengthen the road to realizing your dreams. You can also increase the number of obstacles in your path and the amount of effort it will take you to redirect your life back to the direction you want to travel.

Of all of our possessions, wisdom alone is immortal."

—Isocrates (436-338 BC)

Wisdom can help you find the best solutions by providing you with an abundance of information that you can relate to similar circumstances. It will allow you to see many angles of a problem in order to locate the correct solution. You must be willing to allow wisdom to do its job. You have it. You can't get rid of it. You might as well use it the way nature intended for you to use it.

Each time you use knowledge learned in a previous life lesson, you build upon it. That adds yet another dimension to your problem-solving skills and makes your possible outcomes even more desirable. So stop ignoring the wisdom chest, and use it.

"Don't gain the world and lose your soul, Wisdom is better than silver or gold."

—Bob Marley (1945-1981)

Use our workbook to help you with your wisdom search at *www. NaturalSuccessPrinciples.com/workbook*.

Chapter Thirty-One

Learn How to Suck

When Jonna was born, she didn't know how to suckle from a bottle or nipple. Even though this is an automatic reflex in most full-term babies, it is an involuntary action that does not show up until the baby is almost full-term before birth. Therefore, Jonna was born too early to have developed this vital reflex that has a huge bearing on a baby's survival.

She had to have a feeding tube inserted while she was taught to suck. She had to have a special bottle because her mouth was too tiny to nurse. Even her mother's nipple was too big for her tiny mouth.

The importance of this is that Jonna had to learn to suck, and you should too. Not literally, of course, but it is relevant when you consider that many of life's vital functions are learned behaviors that enable us to grow. Learn those things that can assist you, no matter how automatic you think they should be. If they haven't worked for you up to this point, then learn them again. It may be possible that you didn't quite catch it the first time around. Reinvent what you think you know; you may be surprised by the outcome.

For instance, if you have been trying to sell yourself on your resume to a company or field that continuously rejects your efforts, redo the resume. Find out why it isn't working. Adjust your approach so that it will work for you. The art of presenting yourself in a positive light on a resume is a learned and necessary skill for gaining ground in today's world. Make it work for you by learning what changes you need to make. At NaturalSuccessPrinciples.com, we can help with all aspects of your resume. We can get you in contact with people who help you.

If you are trying to get into a college that keeps telling you your application isn't well-rounded enough for acceptance, find out what is missing, and fix it. Learn what is expected, then go after it. Get well-rounded and add to it. I'll bet the results you get the next time you submit your application will be different.

If you're a writer and you only receive rejections, ask for details. Most editors will give you specific reasons why your work is not getting published. Take that information and use it just as Jonna took what she learned and applied it to eating. She learned how to suck. Don't you think it's time you did, too?

Use our workbook to help you with your reinvention at *www. NaturalSuccessPrinciples.com/workbook.*

Chapter Thirty-Two

Four Feet Crushes More Grapes

Only a fool can't see that in order to overcome a set of circumstances, utilizing people whose strengths are your weaknesses will balance the entire situation. The right people in the right place with the right attitudes can make a difference between success and failure. Surrounding yourself with good people who are team players can also make the difference between your Natural Success Principles being used and losing the ability to focus on the task at hand.

I know I haven't mentioned my wife much during Jonna's journey, but make no mistake; she was an extremely integral part of it all. In fact, if she hadn't been there and hadn't taken an active role in Jonna's care, Jonna would have had a decreased chance of survival. However, I don't pretend to know my wife's innermost thoughts, and I have refrained from trying to do so. It would only get me in trouble, and it wouldn't be fair to her, as she is a bright and intelligent woman who has a right to speak her own mind.

My wife read and researched with me on too many occasions to count. She gave just as many hours and as much, if not more, of herself to help Jonna survive as I did. We discovered the best course of action we could take together. In the process, we grew even closer together than we had been.

Many couples have a hard time coming to terms with the difficulty of having a child who is premature. The stress is tremendous, and the inclination to place blame erroneously on one another is horrifically tempting, especially on the bad days when your child is struggling to survive and you are being prepared for the worst.

In the case of me and my wife, that didn't happen. We had always been deeply committed to one another and extremely close. Our bonds strengthened even more in our efforts to help our infant daughter in her fight to survive.

We discovered that there was nothing better than breast milk for an infant. It offered more protection against disease and more nutrition in a more digestible form than any commercial formula could have. With this discovery, my wife took the initiative and pumped her breast milk every three hours without fail. She did it so that we had a supply for Jonna that would be sufficient for her needs. She strived to make sure she did everything in her power as a mother to increase her daughter's chances of survival even when that effort completely drained her.

As with all mothers who have just given birth, my wife was tired and sore, but she never complained. If the situation had required it, she would have gladly pumped her breast milk every hour for the sake of our child.

How does this tie into your success? It's simple, really. Not only must you surround yourself with people who exude success, you must also be surrounded by good people who compliment you in whatever you are doing that you want to succeed in to reach your goals. It takes more than just yourself sometimes, and you must be able to recognize that.

If you are in business and it begins to fail, you need to be looking for the guy who has a similar business and find out what he's doing that you're not if he's finding success in it. You need to discover how to use the strengths of every single person on your team and how to make those strengths work for you. You should be trying to learn every bit of the information you come across that shows a promise of turning that business around. Then you need to apply what you learn.

It isn't good enough to simply say, "My business is failing. There's nothing I can do." There is always something you can do, even if it is only learning for the next time you try. Never should you just give in and quit. Sometimes in the process of searching for the answers to your business woes, you will come across the solution that will turn your failing business into a thriving one in the blink of an eye.

If you've tried to write a song and have the lyrics but can't get the music written, then find someone who can write the music for your lyrics. Work together to discover the solution to your success. Make it work. Get the right people in the right places at the right time and you will be unstoppable in your pursuit of success.

"It is literally true that you can succeed best and quickest by helping others to succeed."

—Napoleon Hill (1883-1970)

If you have been itching to write a book but have no idea how to begin or if you know that you aren't proficient in prose, guess what you must do? That's right—you must find someone who can balance you. You must find a person who is strong in prose who can articulate your ideas in a way that is uniquely yours. Get the right writer to help you get your thoughts on paper in an appealing manner and you will have placed the right person in the right place. We can help you at NaturalSuccessPrinciples.com. We can get you started on your story and get you published as well. We are eliminating the excuses of everyone's success.

If you have a house to sell and don't know where to find a buyer, find the right realtor. Find the person who fills the professional need. You must continue on your forward march to your success and get them on your team. Invest in building your team of people for every situation in life.

Before you start screaming, "I can't afford to do that! You haven't seen my bank account," calm down. It doesn't have to be a financial investment. In most cases, the investment is time. Spend time cultivating relationships with the people who are necessary in your quest for success. Get involved with them. Make them your allies. You need them for your success.

What do they get out of it? I think I heard someone whisper that under their breath. The people you surround yourself with for the purpose of balancing your strengths and weaknesses in any given venture get the same thing out of it as you do: Success. You will find that your idea of success and your goals will match those that you surround yourself with during the phases of your success. Each provides the balance the other needs. Both find success or the next step of their journey filled by the association you form.

For example, a writer who wants to be published will surround himself with those who can assist in that goal. That may include editors, publishers, readers of the genre he wishes to publish, and those who will encourage his efforts even in times of difficulty.

A doctor will not remain solitary. He will search out nurses, patients, and colleagues for professional development who will provide him with the means to reach his goal of helping others through illness.

A computer programmer will find a software company and executives as well as project managers, graphic designers, marketers, and other relevant professionals for his means if he intends to sell an idea for a new type of software for the betterment of technology.

In short, you will seek those who can elevate you to your goals through mutual need and common goals that cement the relationship between the parties involved. You must make sure that the people you choose are good people who are diligent in their efforts to succeed in the joint venture.

Use our workbook to help you with your team at *www. NaturalSuccessPrinciples.com/workbook.*

Chapter Thirty-Three

Playing Chicken In The Pool Makes A Difference

We are natural-born helpers. As children we scramble to help in every way possible, even when our help is making a mound of work for our parents. We want to wash the dishes, do the laundry, mow the lawn, and scrub the toilet. We try to help make breakfast, although we often forget at that age to use a skillet when making eggs.

All anyone around us at that stage has to do to get us to help is make the merest suggestion of allowing us to help. If Dad's outside under the truck changing the oil and says he may need someone to hand him tools, we're there. If Mom is cleaning out the closets and wonders aloud how she will place the items into a large pile, we're on it.

We don't have to know what we are doing or be coaxed into it with payment. We'll work for free, a hug, a kiss, or a Tootsie Roll just as quickly as we would have for a hundred dollar bill. We don't worry about getting it right; we only want to help.

Our parents encourage this by forgetting to mention the mistakes we made during our help session. Dad may have a large bump on his forehead from us dropping a wrench on it, but he never says so. Mom may have had to get up in the middle of the night and completely redo our sorting job in the closet, but she doesn't mention it. Instead, Mom and Dad praise us for our efforts and encourage us to continue to help.

As we grow older, we discover something. People take advantage of those who are too willing and eager to help. People are critical of the help we give. We begin to withdraw our eagerness to be of assistance. Our tender hearts don't want to hear the cruel words about the help we give, and we don't want to give up all of our time for someone who won't do it for themselves.

The desire we have to help gets buried and forgotten. We resist helping after that, and Mom and Dad now must argue with us to get us to do anything, from picking up our own clothes to taking our dishes to the sink. We begin to hide yet another of our inborn principles in an effort to protect it.

How can this be, you ask? Well, it's really just as simple as that. Humans are social creatures with a need and drive to help each other. The need to help and build a system of leadership based on the help and skills of everyone in a particular group of humans has been well documented throughout history. Some of the best documentation comes from the dawn of man.

In those societies, many of the principles we have been talking about throughout this book were displayed openly. They depended upon the use of natural success to create a life in which the society could flourish. We have, with the introduction of a new definition of success over the course of thousands of years, thrown out their fundamental beliefs and created a society that does not encourage us to use what we already have.

What we need to do is release that willingness to help others. Get involved in some form of volunteer work. Do something nice for someone just because they could use a hand. Help others with the same joy that you had when you were a child.

Helping someone else does more than make you look good. It gives you the opportunity to build upon every other Natural Success Principle we've talked about and to incorporate that into your success. Helping others gives you the chance to be put in contact with those whose goals depend upon a hand from another at that moment in time.

My goal is to make prematurity very visible and understood. We lose too many children from it. I started the Early Journey Foundation to do that. I couldn't find a cause that I believed in so strongly after

Jonna's birth, so I created it. I want other families who are facing the same journey we had with Jonna to have the support and assistance they may need regardless of their income level. I want each child who is born prematurely to have the same opportunities as Jonna did. I also started the world's first social network for PreeMiracles and those who love them at PreeMiracles.com. My other creation was Natural Success Principles, LLC. This company is where I am going to eliminate the excuses anyone has for success if they just come in and listen. This book is just the start.

If your beliefs lead you to your cause, then go after it. Otherwise find a cause and start helping today. The more you help others, the more benefits you reap. Benefits equal success, people. Helping gives change a kick in the behind to get it moving in your life and in the lives of others.

Go get involved and release your natural desire to help. Let that desire out of the bag and into your life. Make a difference. Anyone can live life, but it takes someone special to make a difference in that life. Be that someone special.

Everyone talks of those fifteen minutes of fame. If you want true fame, the kind that matters at the end of the day, then help others. It may not bring you massive financial rewards. It may not even bring you a plaque with your name on it, but it will make a positive influence in your life and in the lives of the people you help along the way. You will have learned to let their success be its own reward because the payments are far more lasting than any money one can make.

Use our workbook to help you with your helping at *www. NaturalSuccessPrinciples.com/workbook.*

Chapter Thirty-Four

Hey, Get This—You Really Have to Get Off the Couch!

Now that we've discussed all of the Natural Success Principles and you know that you must take responsibility, visualize, remain positive, help, and a whole bunch of other things along the way, you need to know that there is one thing that must happen for any of the others to fall into place: You must work.

I have never seen one single thing occur from thought alone. I didn't just think about Jonna's situation. I worked to make it better. I didn't just think about writing a book. I didn't only see my daughter at home or me giving seminars, signing copies of my books, or helping others who have premature children through the Early Journey Foundation. I worked for all of these things. I spent hours working at them, trying to make sure I got it right, making sure success would come.

Work isn't easy, and it's not as fun as going into a balloon factory every day or getting to eat candy and play games all day. It is tedious, it is thought provoking, and it is hard. Work, though, is the second-largest success principle that I must offer you. Responsibility only comes first because it is necessary in order to understand that you must work.

If you can read this book and say, "That's too hard, that takes too much time, that isn't much fun," then you have wasted your time and mine at this point. Put this book down and give up. Don't email me or participate in anything that I do. I can't help you.

But before you do give up, think about this: You bought this book. You looked for ways to improve your life. You wanted, on some level, to better yourself. Why would you do all of that and then place that effort that you took at the bottom of garbage dumpster?

Success isn't easy. No one is going to hand it to you on a silver platter. No one is going to bail you out, although you may be tossed a few lifelines along the way. You must work at it, and that takes time and sweat.

When someone comes up to you and says that success is the easiest thing in the world, you now know this to be true. First, think of what your definition of success has become as you have read this book. Next think about the fact that if success were so very easy to achieve within your definition of it, why haven't you done it thus far?

You haven't done it because you didn't realize you already had the tools for success built in. You didn't realize how to use those tools. You didn't know the very things you needed to build success were hidden inside you and had been there since before you were born.

However, tools alone are not enough. A mechanic's tools cannot fix a problem with a car if they remain hidden in his toolbox. He must take them out and apply them. He has to physically and mentally use them in order for those tools to do what they are supposed to do.

A doctor cannot perform surgery without the proper tools and equipment. What this book has attempted to do is to give you the necessary equipment to fix your life and give you the opportunity to succeed. Before you can succeed, you needed to know to look inside your toolbox. Then you needed to know how each tool could be used. Finally, you must begin working with the tools you have, the Natural Success Principles within you, and apply them to the areas in your life which are your goals where they can help you reach success.

If you need to give work another name in order to become motivated to do it, then by all means, rename it. After all, Shakespeare did imply that a rose by any other name would smell as sweet. The name you give work isn't important. Your attitude toward work is.

"Get happiness out of your work or you may never know what happiness is."

—Elbert Hubbard (1856-1915)

You must commit yourself to working each day on your success and making that work count. Build a little more on what you did the day before. Keep your focus and continue even when it's hard. There are going to be hard times in the middle of what seems so simple in concept. The concepts are simple; the path isn't always free of brambles.

Anytime something is worth wanting, it is worth working toward. The effort spent always has more rewards than the initial investment that is placed into it. Success is something that many want, is definitely worth having regardless of your definition for success, and always yields a higher return than the time, sweat, tears, skinned knees, and bruised egos put into it during the investment stage. However, you will only see that return if you remain committed to success and work for it.

I can't stress to you enough how important working is. Working for what you want makes it have a much sweeter taste when you reach the goal you have toiled over for so long. There is nothing that can compare to it. Jonna's journey to survival and getting to come home was pure ecstasy because of the work that had been done to make it happen. It was the reward for everything we went through in the 130 days of uncertainty. Her homecoming was our payment for sticking it out, for learning, for changing, for becoming parents, and for appreciating the chance we had been given.

If you want to feel that kind of success, then you must work to get it. Work until you think you can't work anymore. Try and keep trying when nothing seems to go right for you. Make success happen by working toward it with a persistence and tenacity that would place the fear of God in God himself. Earn your success.

Use our workbook to help you with your work rewards at *www. NaturalSuccessPrinciples.com/workbook*.

Chapter Thirty-Five

Only You Can Prevent Your Failure

The most important thing for you to realize and to burn into your mind at this time is that the whole process of using your Natural Success Principles falls squarely on your shoulders and no place else. This doesn't mean you must do it completely alone, as you may need to search for people who can help you, mentor you, and give you guidance.

It's okay to look for books, attend seminars, and locate activities that launch you into your journey of success. I encourage you to read, attend and complete activities for success. It takes a lot of reminders and alarms to get you off the snooze button of your life. It's normal to search out that which will show you how, give you hope, and encourage you along the way. It's perfectly fine to talk about your goals, visualize your goals, and dream of your goals. These things are necessary to prepare you for success.

What isn't alright is to assume that someone else will apply what you find to your life and that it will magically materialize into your success. The entire process of application and responsibility for your new knowledge to your current situation is on you. Only you can change you. Only you know if you want success badly enough. Your entire quest is inside you and no one else. You and you alone are responsible for you. No one else can be.

All of the governments, books, seminars, mentors, and societies of the world are powerless to help you unless you want to be helped. You are the only one with the power to realize your potential and the only one to whom it matters enough to change, to care. If I can get you to understand one thing and one thing only, it would be that you hold all of the responsibility for your life and what happens in it or to it.

There is nothing more vital to your quest for success than to realize that you must take full responsibility for every little thing you do. Every action you take is your responsibility. Every reaction that your action causes, every reaction you have to someone else's actions, is your responsibility.

Every thought you have determines who you are. What you do, how you act, how you react—everything. There is nothing that you experience in life that cannot be traced directly back to you and your decisions. As such, you must be careful in how you conduct yourself, and be ready to accept whatever it is that comes as a direct result of the decisions you have made. You are exactly where you want to be right now. I know that is hard to swallow, but you are the exact product of your decisions.

If you don't like the way your decisions are turning out, you must change the way you make decisions. No one can do it for you. You must—only you. It all comes down to helping yourself and being committed to improving yourself every day of your life.

I'm not saying you won't stumble along the way or that when you do experience a setback you can't pick yourself up. I am saying that when you fall, don't expect someone on a white horse to ride up and save you. If you want to be saved, get up and save yourself.

To save yourself, to reach success and realize the power that accomplishment brings to you, you must work. You must pick yourself up and start again when the cards fall against the breeze. You must reevaluate your goals and your definition of success. You should decide what steps must be taken, and then make the decision to take them.

Natural Success Principles only work and can only be accessed when you take your wisdom chest out and use it wisely. You must work at it every day, and you must find the best solutions for your circumstances yourself. The Natural Success Principles that I have introduced are not new to you. They are and always have been a part of you. You were born with them, are entitled to them, and deserve to use them to reach your full potential.

I can present the information, wrap it up in a nice little book, and deliver it to your hands by way of a bookstore. I cannot make you use the knowledge you have gained, force you to set goals, fix your situation for you, or hand you success on a silver platter. I can only serve up what I have discovered to be true within us all and hope that you take up the plate and eat from it.

I cannot even make your sorry butt get off the couch and change the channel, much less your life.

If you have the desire, the drive, and the confidence to think and to believe, then you will reach the place in your life that you seek. You will find your personal idea of success and begin to live it. You will discover the Natural Success Principles that were inside you before you were born.

Use our workbook to help you get your sorry tail moving towards success at *www.NaturalSuccessPrinciples.com/workbook*.

Chapter Thirty-Six

Read This Chapter Without Buying the Book

This chapter, above all else, is the one you want to read. If you cannot buy the book, read this one chapter now to change your life forever. The concept presented here will get you more motivated than any other concept anywhere else on the planet. If it fails in this aspect, I weep for you. No one can help you if you do not grasp the concept in this chapter. Not one person. If you cannot get rid of what is holding you back, I cannot replace it with new thoughts. Look deep inside right now.

It is at birth and before that you are like all of the other creatures on earth. You are incapable of making conscious decisions that crush your true potential. Take this fact to heart right now. Not one other creature on this planet refuses to take responsibility for their survival or to be the best or biggest they can be. You only learn to make decisions that hinder your true success as you grow.

"I hate mankind, for I think myself one of the best of them, and I know how bad I am."

—Joseph Baretti (1716-1789)

As you grasp this concept, I can hear some of you starting to spout out euphemisms for "higher species." "This is what makes us superior to the other animals of the earth, compassion, rational thought, and the desire for equality."

Let's take recent events—men with tigers, woman with chimpanzee, all with disastrous outcomes. It came to a point where the animal desired to be the top dog.

Trees grow as tall and big as they can. They don't limit themselves at all. Wind breaks a branch, the tree grows another, there is a year of drought, and next year the tree drinks double.

We are the only species that limits ourselves, not only from our conscious decisions, but limits others with pettiness, class envy, and jealousy.

I see people everyday who tear down successful people: "He's too rich." "Get more blood from that turnip." "Oh, fancy pants in her big house."

Jealousy is ugly.

"Man is the only animal that blushes. Or needs to."
—Mark Twain (1835-1910)

Instead of tearing down others, find a way to lift yourself up. Read and learn new skills to improve your position in a company. Find ways to save or make more so you can buy a bigger house. Don't make someone lower so you feel superior.

Don't look to others to stop succeeding so you can be lazy.

In fact, this is the best thing I saw in my daughter. She accepted every negative thrown her way and fought to be the biggest and best she could be. She did everything perfectly.

She grew new branches.

Why would you look to others for your success?

The next sentence is the cold, hard fact. Get ready, you are either going to continue to drone on in your life, or you will change forever from this one sentence. Prepare yourself, everything will change. Once this knowledge gets out, we will know which of our species is a failure and which of our species wishes to succeed. Here it is:

No one—not your mother, father, co-worker, boss, aunt, uncle, brother, sister, priest, rabbi, policeman, fireman, postman, grandparents, store clerk, internet email, president, government, congress, free money, bailout, loan, Nicaraguan bank manager, lottery, book, motivational speaker, coach, sports team, or animal can make you successful or is responsible to make you successful. Only you are as an individual.

Let's look at something else. We actually make laws or regulations that diminish or punish or inhibit success in some way.

Why? Does it make us feel better?

For some reason everyone is thinking that we are all owed the same thing no matter our input amount.

Look at this example:

One guy works for twenty years, saves, invests, and betters himself through a lifetime of learning.

Another is a dropout, holds jobs for only weeks, stops learning, saves nothing, but *expects the same rewards and lifestyle as the guy above!*

This is where the argument earlier in this chapter that we are superior because of our equal thinking ends. We have long since passed where this argument holds water.

We cannot continue allowing the second person to even exist. (Oh my, did he just say that?) Yes. Nothing in nature has ever done this. If it did so, dinosaurs would all be laying around eating only what they planted themselves, and one of them would be planting nothing and still expect to eat.

Do you understand how ridiculous this concept is now?

This mindset is the most destructive concept that is plaguing our society; nigh, our very existence.

I feel sorry for the second guy. He has buried his Natural Success Principles. I wish to help him, but alas, I cannot. No one can help if he continues with such a devastating frame of mind.

Here is the bad part—these thoughts need to become extinct. That thinking is not conducive to nature or survival and especially not to success. There is no equality other than that we all have the same set of principles I have laid out in this book. Since we all have them, we can all achieve more. Some people have chosen to use them, and some people have chosen to bury them.

So let's delve even deeper—the unemployment rate in our nation will never be zero. Want to know why?

Some people are unemployable. Got it. Some people choose *not* to either work or work to the best of their ability.

Is it fair to give them what others have produced? Does this not perpetuate failure? Does this not increase the layers which are piled upon your Natural Success Principles so that you will not see them or use them and become dependent on someone or something—usually the government?

If you are one of these people, I swear I want to help you break free. You can never be successful when you are dependent on others. We need to break the addiction to your own failure.

"Just because you got the monkey off your back doesn't mean the circus has left town."

—George Carlin (1937- 2008)

Use our workbook to help you with your individuality at *www. NaturalSuccessPrinciples.com/workbook.*

Chapter Thirty-Seven

The American Chapter

This chapter is very dear to me. America. We live in the greatest country that has ever been placed on this earth. I know this book will be read in hundreds of countries, and I will speak in hundreds of countries. I do have to speak only on what I know and what I grew up to know. I am sorry if you live in a country that has forces to hold down your Natural Success. I am sorry if you are barricading yourself in failure. I just know that here, nothing will stop you if you are willing to work hard.

My father was in the Air Force for most of my young life; in fact, I was born in Turkey. After twenty-two years in the military, he spent twenty years in civil service on an Air Force base. I have been brought up to realize what it takes to keep this country safe. I have never had a tiny fraction of a thought that this is not the greatest country on earth.

We have done so much in so little time. Our history is very short, yet imagine at the greatness we have accomplished! Without American ingenuity, look at the amount of babies like mine who would not have lived. Without American inventors like Philo T. Farnsworth, inventor of the Isolette, my child might not have made it. There is nothing—and I mean nothing—that can't be accomplished in America.

One thing that I always noticed about people is that they always will speak fairly well about their family. Even if they have a loved one who is a screw-up, most people will defend their family member to the bitter end. Look at wives defending husbands who just beat them. Look at parents defending children who just committed a crime. There is a blind allegiance to the family member regardless of the situation. Everyone else is wrong.

Can someone then explain to me how we have people who blame America first? Explain to me how you don't feel like part of the American family when you are here. Please give me the reasons to say that we, as a country that is the epitome of success as far as countries go, still have persons who talk down this country. I will fight for her. I will bleed for her. She is my family member.

Once you grasp this concept, listening to anyone talk bad about America should turn on a red light. This person is no longer in the family. Understand that I am not saying that we should not look for better ways, better paths, and better life, but let's not tear down what we have to do it. Remember, tearing down something for your success is wrong. Why tear down America to feel better about yourself?

America is the greatest, and your country can be also. The more people we have who understand these Principles given to you *before* you were born, the better this planet will be.

I sit here now and vow to you that if you uncover your principles written in this book, you will be far greater and achieve more than you have ever dreamed.

I promise that each day will be the greatest day, and each moment will be the greatest moment.

True Success is doing what you *want* to do at any given moment.

Afterword

Now that every tool for your success is known to you, along with the knowledge that these tools are already yours, I hope you take up the challenge to succeed. There is nothing to buy to succeed. You can't find success in a bulk email. You won't find it hiding inside a closet somewhere. The government won't mail it to you in a stimulus check. You already own it. You only have to realize it.

It may take an event in your life that changes everything you thought you believed in to get you motivated enough to take control. It did for me. Jonna is the reason I finally realized I already had everything I needed. I didn't know that before she came along.

Prior to Jonna, I thought success was the same as society's idea of it. I thought it was making money, building bank accounts, and padding a retirement fund. I thought the way you obtained success was through investments and very carefully planned and choreographed business deals.

What I discovered is that success is a way of life, a belief system that is unshakable. Success is being Jonna's father. It is being a husband, a provider, and a good person. Success is learning in everything I do, in supporting my wife in everything she does, and in ensuring my daughter never has anything cover up her Success stores. It is nurturing my daughter so that she grows up well-balanced and stable. Success isn't money. Success is how I feel about myself and those I love.

It took a tiny baby to show me that simple fact. It took being backed up against the wall with my hands tied and being desperate to save something that I had helped create through the love my wife and I share. Before then, I had lived in a dream and missed the reality of the world around me.

Jonna brought me back to the present moment in one wrenching moment that lasted 130 days. She gave me back the joy that is life and placed all of my perceived difficulties in perfect perspective. No longer did I think that I wasn't a success if I didn't make the next big technological move in the region. Technology became a passion again, something that I enjoy doing, but not the reason I live my life. Jonna helped me to see what a great wife I have and to focus more on nurturing my wife, because I don't ever want to lose her. Jonna taught me that there is a love that has strength beyond any other form. She taught me how to really love another in a way I didn't know was possible.

As I continue my journey with the people in my life, I continue to learn and readjust my idea of success. Jonna is still teaching me how to really live and what is really important in life. She will always have the ability to teach me.

The angel God sent me to call my own earned her wings upon her birth. I'm still working on mine. Now I know I must earn those wings, because I will need to be able to fly with Jonna when she decides to spread her wings and test the currents of the soaring breeze.

Every morning I wake and I know that today will be a successful day. I know because Jonna has given me the keys to my own Natural Success. No matter what happens, I know I can succeed. No matter how tough it gets, it is perfect. I am alive. I feel the breath in my lungs, the breeze on my skin, and Jonna's kisses on my cheek. As long as I am alive, life is perfect. That's the true beauty of realizing your Natural Success Principles.

You now understand why I must share these principles around the world. I must get this knowledge to humanity as fast as possible.

It is now my life.

About The Author

A dedication to hard work and his years of "sweat" equity and you would already have a powerful mentor.

Then something happened.

The birth of his daughter.

In his first book, Blessed With Tragedy – A Father's Journey With His PreeMiracle, Jack tells the story in day-by-day diary format written while in the struggle for life and death with his daughter Jonna. From the smallest teacher, one father learns the greatest lessons in life. Her example continues to inspire him as she beat the odds stacked against her, one miraculous moment at a time.

Jack is now on a speaking tour and unleashing the power within at his motivational seminars. He is available for appearances. You may request him at www.JackHatfield.com.

He founded the Early Journey Foundation, a non-profit organization that is the frontline for parents of PreeMiracles the world over. He has also created and developed the World's First and Largest Social Networking Website dedicated to PreeMiracles and those who love them. Visit www.PreeMiracles.com and join the community that is facing unique challenges and that together we can help them all.

His life has changed and he is determined to make a difference in the lives of as many people as possible.

His company, Natural Success Principles, LLC at www.NaturalSuccessPrinciples.com is focused and dedicated on helping people uncover their true passion, work towards their goals, and be the success they wish to be. His speeches, websites, and personal coaching will be the definitive difference in the lives of so many people. He has gathered other mentors and put together a motivational package all at www.AnytimeSuccess.com which will help you on a daily basis.

"I have said that I will not allow my daughter's lessons sit stagnate, and I promise I want to help you succeed with this wisdom. Let's grow right now together."

Your Special Invitation

I know you can't believe the book and your trip with me has ended. I am here to tell you it has not.

If you want the whole prelude, it is in the incredible book *Blessed with Tragedy: A Father's Journey with his PreeMiracle.*

Order it at *www.BlessedwithTragedy.com* or wherever books are sold. Proceeds from that book go to two non-profits helping families of premature babies.

To find out more on me, follow me on Twitter, and read my blog, go to *www.JackHatfield.com.* Keep track to find out when I am in your area, and please come see me.

To donate to my foundation, go to *www.EarlyJourneyFoundation.org.*

To join the World's First and Largest Social Network for PreeMiracles and those who love them, go to *www.PreeMiracles.com.*

To help parents of PreeMiracles, go to *www.Preemieqs.com.*

Now for the super stuff:

I understand this is a lot to absorb. I want to help you.

Use our workbook to help you with your emergence at *www. NaturalSuccessPrinciples.com/workbook.*

This workbook is the crucial component to getting you to reach inside yourself deeper than reading can. It is putting your thoughts to paper and making a commitment to change.

I wish to help everyone achieve their greatest potential. Since you purchased this book, you are going to get a sweet deal. You can get my ten step mini-course absolutely free. Yes, free.

http://www.NaturalSuccessPrinciples.com/bookbuyerfreebie

It holds with it another special surprise.

If you wish to eliminate your excuses for success and everything else, come join us at *www.NaturalSuccessPrinciples.com.*

What If, with One Book, You Could....

Help Parents Struggling with the new task of child survival?
Raise awareness of the Number One killer of newborns?
Positively impact Neonatal Units as they prepare for more and more children?

The Early Journey Foundation was formed to bring forth the ever-growing plight of prematurity to the forefront of knowledge. Being thrust into the world of prematurity, our founder saw a need as he looked around the NICU and saw other families coping with the stresses of giving birth early.

Someone has to help right now. With your help, we can make a difference. We help parents right now by giving away knowledge and support. When a parent gives birth to a new PreeMiracle™, we send books, bottles, blankets, and mobiles to the parents so they can be armed with knowledge and have the items they need. We have them join the World's First Social Network for premature parents. We give them a website blog where they can post information and photos to update other family members. We help them immediately.

Please support our cause with a simple donation or purchase.

Every minute of everyday, we are blessed with another premature birth.

Premature births have risen over 20% in the last decade.

In an Average Week in the U.S.

10,056
Babies are born preterm

1,604
are born very preterm

6,511
are born low birthweight

1,188
are born very low birthweight

With your donation as outlined below, you can help give books to those parents and provide them with the other essentials as well. For every case you or your company purchase, you will get a signed copy by the author for you or your company.

Please send out _____ case(s) of books to new PreeMiracle Parents in my behalf @ 252.00 each.
I understand that I help 42 families with each case! This lasts 42 minutes.

In Honor of: _____

Address: _____

City: _____ State: _____ Zip: _____

Email: _____

I AM ENCLOSING A CHECK FOR $_____ PAYABLE TO EARLY JOURNEY FOUNDATION OR PLEASE CHARGE MY CREDIT CARD.

Card Number: _____ Exp Date: _____

Name on Card: _____

Signature: _____

Billing Address: _____

Mail to: Early Journey Foundation ' PO Box 116 Camden SC 29020 '

The Early Journey Foundation is a not-for-profit organization recognized as tax exempt under IRS code 501(c)3. Our mission is to be in the forefront of the battle with prematurity, with parental support and knowledge programs. Your donation is tax deductible.

BUY A SHARE OF THE FUTURE IN YOUR COMMUNITY

These certificates make great holiday, graduation and birthday gifts that can be personalized with the recipient's name. The cost of one S.H.A.R.E. or one square foot is $54.17. The personalized certificate is suitable for framing and will state the number of shares purchased and the amount of each share, as well as the recipient's name. The home that you participate in "building" will last for many years and will continue to grow in value.

Here is a sample SHARE certificate:

YES, I WOULD LIKE TO HELP!

I support the work that Habitat for Humanity does and I want to be part of the excitement! As a donor, I will receive periodic updates on your construction activities but, more importantly, I know my gift will help a family in our community realize the dream of homeownership. **I would like to SHARE in your efforts against substandard housing in my community!** *(Please print below)*

PLEASE SEND ME _____ SHARES at $54.17 EACH = $ $_____

In Honor Of: _____

Occasion: (Circle One)   HOLIDAY   BIRTHDAY   ANNIVERSARY

      OTHER: _____

Address of Recipient: _____

Gift From: _____ *Donor Address:* _____

Donor Email: _____

I AM ENCLOSING A CHECK FOR $ $_____ PAYABLE TO HABITAT FOR HUMANITY OR PLEASE CHARGE MY VISA OR MASTERCARD *(CIRCLE ONE)*

Card Number _____ Expiration Date: _____

Name as it appears on Credit Card _____ Charge Amount $ _____

Signature _____

Billing Address _____

Telephone # Day _____ Eve _____

PLEASE NOTE: Your contribution is tax-deductible to the fullest extent allowed by law.
Habitat for Humanity • P.O. Box 1443 • Newport News, VA 23601 • 757-596-5553
www.HelpHabitatforHumanity.org